Triune Atonement

Christ's Healing for Sinners, Victims, and the Whole Creation

ANDREW SUNG PARK

WJK WESTMINSTER
JOHN KNOX PRESS
LOUISVILLE • KENTUCKY

To Sun-Ok Jane Myong

Book design by Drew Stevens
Cover design by Eric Walljasper, Minneapolis, MN
Cover photo by Tony Schutz
Sculpture by Nicholas Britsky (1914–2005) in St. Patrick's Church, Urbana, Illinois

First edition
Published by Westminster John Knox Press
Louisville, Kentucky

This book is printed on acid-free paper that meets the American National Standards Institute Z39.48 standard. ∞

PRINTED IN THE UNITED STATES OF AMERICA

09 10 11 12 13 14 15 16 17—10 9 8 7 6 5 4 3 2 1

Library of Congress Cataloging-in-Publication Data

Park, Andrew Sung.
  Triune atonement : Christ's healing for sinners, victims, and the whole creation / Andrew Sung Park.
      p. cm.
  Includes bibliographical references and index.
  ISBN 978-0-664-23347-1 (alk. paper)
  1. Atonement. 2. Asian Americans—Religion. I. Title.
  BT265.3.P37 2009
  232'.3—dc22   2008018545

Contents

Preface

Martin Buber said that he was not Christian because Jesus was not the Messiah for whom the Jews had waited. For them, the final goal of the Messiah is "the redemption of Israel and of the world." Buber denied Jesus as the Messiah: "I believe equally firmly that we will never recognize Jesus as the Messiah Come, for this would contradict the deepest meaning of our Messianic passion. In our view redemption occurs forever, and none has yet occurred. Standing, bound and shackled, in the pillory of mankind, we demonstrate with the bloody body of our people the unredeemedness of the world. For us there is no cause of Jesus; only the cause of God exists for us."[1] It is true that since Jesus came to the world we have not seen true peace, but rather much of violence.

What does Jesus' cross bring to humanity? What does it do for us? How does it save us from sins?

My interest in the theme of atonement was inspired by my mother. When I was three years old, a fire broke out in my house. My mother jumped into the burning house to rescue me from the flames. She was burned severely. I deeply thank my mother, Chong-hui Kim, for risking her life to save me and for giving me the chance to live and to reflect on Jesus' atonement. This event eventually led me to wonder how Jesus' death saves victims from their "sins."

This short book is an attempt to explore and clarify the biblical and theological meanings of Jesus' atonement for victims and victimizers from an Asian American perspective. After reviewing major atonement theories, I present the idea of the triune healing that grapples with the problems of sin, wounds (*han*), and ecological disruptions.

The triune atonement refers to the involvement of the Trinity in the atonement for God's creation. Jesus initiated the atonement of the world, and the Paraclete (the Advocate) has continued his work of atonement for the past two thousand years. In this triune atonement, the Paraclete assumes a pivotal role in redeeming humanity and renewing the whole creation. The Paraclete is the Holy Spirit, but in a sense the two are distinguishable. The Holy Spirit that went through all the experiences of Jesus, particularly the crucifixion and the resurrection, is called the "Advocate." In this sense, the Advocate is a key to understanding Jesus' atonement and the Trinity, disclosing the nature of Jesus Christ and God. Jesus' atonement is not his work alone, but his cooperation with God and the Holy Spirit.

Concerning the identity of the Holy Spirit, the Scripture addresses this third person of the Trinity as the Spirit of God (Gen. 41:38; Matt. 3:16; 12:28; Rom. 8:9; 1 Cor. 2:11; 1 Pet. 4:14). The same Spirit is also called the Spirit of Christ (Rom. 8:9), the Spirit of the Son (Gal. 4:6), and the Spirit of Jesus (Acts 16:7). If Jesus' Spirit is separately mentioned from God's Spirit, is it possible that two Holy Spirits, the Spirit of God and the Spirit of Jesus, coexist? The Scripture states that there is only one Holy Spirit. This fact shows that the Holy Spirit turns into the Paraclete after Jesus' resurrection. Thus, the Paraclete is the Holy Spirit.

The Western church has argued for the procession of the Paraclete from both God and Jesus Christ, while the Eastern church has done so for the procession of the Paraclete from God alone. This controversy of *filioque* ("and the son") split the church into two. My intention is not to explain the controversy, but to point out the significance of the work of the Paraclete involving the person of Jesus Christ and God. Since this book highlights the work of the Paraclete, it denotes the engagement of the triune God in the atonement. Therefore, the title of the book is *Triune Atonement*. The term *atonement* in this book includes the salvation of the oppressors, the liberation of the oppressed, and the restoration of nature.

For the publication of this book, I am indebted to several people at the United Theological Seminary. I would like to express my deep gratitude to Tom Boomershine, who read the early manuscript and advised me to change it significantly; Tyron Inbody, who read the entire manuscript and offered insightful comments and encouragement; Larry Welborn, who shared his own understanding of atonement with me; Tom Dozeman, who informed me on the theme of atonement in the Hebrew Bible; Jason Vickers, who encouraged me to include the ecological dimension of atonement; and my research assistants, Cortney Haley and Rebecca Woods, who helped me many ways. I also appreciate Edward Poitras of Perkins School of Theology, who helped me to find resources for this work. My friend Barry Gannon edited this manuscript, sacrificing his holiday time. My editor, Donald McKim, deserves my deep gratitude for editing and publishing this book.

My older son Amos read parts of the manuscript and edited them, and my younger son Thomas shared his insight for the selection of words. Sun-Ok Jane Myong, my wise friend and spouse, has graciously sacrificed her time to support my writing. I am truly grateful for their prayers and ardent support and help.

Introduction

At the 2003 meeting of the American Academy of Religion, there was a session entitled "The Fifteenth Year of Rita Nakashima Brock's *Journeys by Heart*: Reflections on a Christology of Erotic Power." While several persons spoke about the abusive sides of atonement theories and their desire to stop talking about Jesus' blood for our salvation, James Cone emphatically defended the importance of the blood of Jesus for African American communities. For Cone, the cross of Jesus is a very significant symbol for African Americans because the cross and the lynching tree belong together. Cone holds that Jesus was lynched and that Christians are unable to understand the cross until they see it through the image of a lynching tree with African American bodies hanging there.[1]

Since its publication, Brock's *Journeys by Heart* has aroused tremendous interest in many theologians on the various atonement theories. The theme of abused children runs throughout the book as Brock critically examines the satisfaction theory of atonement. Joanne Carlson Brown and Rebecca Parker also contend that the cross of Jesus encourages women to accept patriarchal abuse by teaching redemptive suffering to them in order that they sacrifice themselves for others.[2]

Furthermore, Brock and Parker argue in *Proverbs of Ashes* that Jesus' death was not particularly unique and that the satisfaction theory of atonement is potentially treacherous and hurtful for women Christians in terms of bolstering "virtuous suffering" and "self-sacrificing love."[3]

Womanist theologians find no help from traditional atonement theories for their salvation. Most of them reject the tendency of traditional atonement theories to sacralize victimhood, suffering, and sacrifice. Delores Williams, in *Sisters in the Wilderness,* addresses the fact that black women were forced to be surrogates during slavery in America and that Jesus represents the ultimate surrogate in the substitutionary atonement theory.[4] The exploitation of their bodies through surrogacy removes black women from construing Jesus' work as the model of surrogacy. Williams emphasizes Jesus' redemption through his life rather than through his death.[5] JoAnne Marie Terrell differs from Williams concerning her understanding of the sacrificial dimension of Jesus' death: "Although I may never be required to give up my life for the sake of my ultimate claims, the peculiar efficacy of mother's sacrifice as well as the Christian story prevent me from discarding the idea altogether, particularly the notion of sacrifice as the surrender or destruction of something prized or desirable for the sake of something with higher claim, a potentially salvific notion with communal dimensions that got lost in the rhetorical impetus of the language of surrogacy."[6] Although women's blood loss has been devalued in Christian patriarchal tradition, Terrell affirms that Jesus' own sacramental example makes possible for all people to see the sacred value of women's blood.

On the one hand, some theologians want to avoid mentioning the blood of Jesus for the redemption of humanity because the cross of Jesus has been used for abusing others and for promoting violence in the world. On the other, to millions of people, the cross of Jesus holds deep meaning for grace and salvation. These two positions have their points. The cross of Christianity can be a sign of oppression or a mark of salvation. This depends on how we see the cross. It is, however, inappropriate to discard the symbol of the cross of Jesus because some people have abused it. That is like throwing out the baby with the bathwater. We need to see the cross in the context of Jesus' overall work for the redemption of humanity and the restoration of the whole creation.

Based on the Bible, the triune atonement view reinterprets Jesus' cross in the context of his entire work. There are four salient points in this view. First, Jesus works for the atonement of the oppressors (sinners) and the oppressed (victims). The oppressors need salvation from their sins and the oppressed need liberation from their oppression. Second, Jesus atones for people through his life, death, resurrection, and postresurrection work. Some atonement theories highlight Jesus' life and crucifixion. Others treat Jesus' life, crucifixion, and his resurrection. This triune healing idea includes Jesus' postresurrection atoning work in the form of the Paraclete. The Paraclete is working for the salvation of sinners and the liberation of their victims. We are not dealing with the event that happened two thousand years ago alone. The living Jesus and the Paraclete are presently working for our atonement. Unlike past-oriented atonement views, the triune healing view centers on the breathing salvific and healing work of Jesus Christ and the Paraclete. Third, Jesus saves and liberates not only human beings but also God's whole creation. Jesus' work realizes the original intention of God's creation beyond human redemption. This triune atonement highlights the renewal of God's whole creation. Fourth, this triune atonement involves the Trinity in such a cosmic, salvific, liberative, and renewal work.

"Jesus died for you" is the most significant statement for one-third of the human family. But if you ask Christians how he died for them, they may answer, "He died for my sins by shedding his blood." If you ask them further, "How can a person who lived two thousand years ago die for your present and future sins?" they may be at a loss for an answer.

The cross of Jesus is one of the most popular and visible symbols in the world. However, how the blood of Jesus saves people from their sins is not well understood. In fact, since the beginning of Christianity, Christians have tried to grasp the meaning of Jesus' blood for their salvation. There are several major theories explaining the effect of Jesus' blood. They draw on certain aspects of the Scripture, partially explaining the biblical metaphors of soteriology, the doctrine of salvation. We will survey the traditional atonement theories with some criticisms: the ransom, Christus Victor, satisfaction, moral influence, penal substitution, last scapegoat, and narrative Christus Victor theories. The ransom theory highlights Jesus as our ransom to release us from the bondage of Satan. The Christus Victor theory depicts Jesus as the victor in the battle against the cosmic forces of the devil. The satisfaction theory depicts Jesus as the God-human who satisfied the demand of God for the restoration of justice for the offenses of sinful humanity against God. The moral influence theory tells us that Jesus came to show us God's love and to be an example for our life of love. The penal substitution theory modifies the satisfaction theory by emphasizing Jesus' death as the penalty paid to God for our sins. The contemporary last scapegoat theory states that Jesus came as the last scapegoat to end the violence of the scapegoating mechanism of society. The narrative Christus Victor theory, based on the Christus Victor theory, stresses the nonviolent nature of Jesus' atonement work.

Supported by certain biblical passages, most traditional theories focus on the salvation of perpetrators or sinners. But what about the healing and liberation of the sinned-against or victims through the blood of Jesus? Was Jesus concerned about helping the sinned-against? In his life and death, Jesus truly cared about victims and the downtrodden. After briefly examining traditional and current atonement theories, we will discuss the triune healing view that delves into the liberation and salvation of humankind and creation.

Regarding the redemption of humanity, sinners and victims need to take two different routes for their salvation and liberation. Sinners need salvation: sin → guilt → repentance → forgiveness → justification by faith → sanctification → entire sanctification (a salvation journey). Victims need liberation: wounds → shame → challenge → forgiving → justice by faith → healing → jubilee (a liberation journey). I have explained these two routes in detail elsewhere.[7] These journeys of liberation and salvation converge at the abundant life Jesus promised.

Jesus comes that sinners and victims may have life abundantly (John 10:10).[8] In Greek, the term "abundant" is *perisson*—exceeding some number or measure or rank or need over and above, more than is necessary. To the Jews, the life that

Moses offered through the law gave them delight (Ps. 1:2). The life Jesus offers is abundant.[9]

Most individuals are sinners as well as those who have been sinned against, and therefore need both salvation and liberation. However, there are some distinctions between the group of sinners and the group of victims. The dividing lines can generally be drawn according to race, gender, and class. Jesus particularly cares about the downtrodden and the marginalized.

At this collective level, Christ's work conspicuously focuses on the liberation and healing of the downtrodden. He came to call "so-called" sinners, who were the victims of religious legalism and social discrimination, such as shepherds, butchers, tanners, the sick, and the Gentiles. Just as Moses led Israelites to the promised land, Jesus liberated the downtrodden from their bondage.

He also served the oppressors by confronting, transforming, and forgiving their wrongs and injustices. For example, he cared enough for the salvation of the rich by challenging a rich young ruler to give away his wealth to follow him. Jesus cared about his true well-being. He also accepted the dinner invitation of Simon the Pharisee and directly confronted his shortcomings (Luke 7:40). He strived to save sinners from their own sins: greed, hubris, injustice, oppression, exploitation, and deception.

As seen in his life, Christ's atoning work was not done as a transaction between God and Satan or between God and Christ, but it was done as the restoration of right relationships between sinners and the sinned-against, through which it bears the fruition of the right relationship between God and humanity. Jesus came to fulfill the original bliss of God's creation so that we may enjoy God's abundant life. Jesus' atonement for the abundant life is not limited to religious redemption but is extended to all aspects of life: economic, political, social, cultural, and ecological.

He came for blessings of all creation. The church needs to see the goal of Jesus' mission in a larger context, to reinterpret it in the public arena, and to pursue it in the public arena. In the present context where the meaning of Jesus' suffering has been misconstrued and abused, it is our urgent task to articulate its true meaning stated in the Bible.

Furthermore, the church has focused on the death and resurrection of Jesus Christ in terms of explaining his atonement work. His redemptive work, however, must not stop at his resurrection. Even after his resurrection, Jesus has continued his redemptive work. Jesus promised that he would send the Paraclete to us after his ascension. The Paraclete came at Pentecost and has carried on Jesus' work, illuminating the meaning of the blood of Jesus in history. The Paraclete is another Jesus (John 14:16). The church has not explicitly explained the work of the Paraclete for our atonement, but God has transformed, saved, and liberated people through the Paraclete. The Paraclete has taken up the mission of Jesus for the past two thousand years by liberating victims, leading sinners to repentance, and restoring God's creation through the symbol of Jesus' cross. This triune healing view is to explore the atoning work of the Paraclete.

The church has also focused on the redemptive work of Jesus Christ for humanity alone. His work surpasses the redemption of humanity, intending the restoration of the whole creation. The risen Christ has relentlessly striven to let God be all in all (1 Cor. 15:28). We will lift up the significance of Jesus' work for the whole creation in the form of the Paraclete.

PART 1

Atonement History

In ancient Judaism, atonement was done through the rituals of sacrifice in the temple. However, the Jews thought that they were saved because they were descendants of Abraham. Through the rituals of atonement, only their transgressions were forgiven.

In Christianity, atonement meant salvation by the work of Jesus Christ. It was for both the forgiveness and the salvation of sinners. In this section, we will survey major atonement theories developed in the course of church history. Each theory will include its main points explained, with primary resources and some evaluations.

The Ransom Theory

According to the *Oxford English Dictionary*, the term *ransom* means "the action of procuring the release of a prisoner or captive by paying a certain sum, or of obtaining one's own freedom in this way; the fact or possibility of being set free on this condition; the paying of money to this end." This ransom theory is based on these New Testament passages:

> Whoever wishes to be first among you must be your slave; just as the Son of Man came not to be served but to serve, and to give his life a ransom for many. (Matt. 20:27–28)

> For the Son of Man came not to be served but to serve, and to give his life a ransom for many. (Mark 10:45)

> For you were bought with a price; therefore glorify God in your body. (1 Cor. 6:20)

> For there is one God; there is also one mediator between God and humankind, Christ Jesus, himself human, who gave himself a ransom for all—this was attested at the right time. (1 Tim. 2:5–6)

This atonement theory upholds the idea that Satan had control over humanity. God paid a ransom to Satan and released humanity from Satan's grip. This theory dominated the church from its early days until the development of Anselm's satisfaction theory.

A number of scholars raise the question about the rights of Satan over humanity. What do we owe to Satan? Some early church fathers believed that sin had human beings subjugated under the dominion of Satan.

3

In the second century, Irenaeus regarded the atonement as the deliverance from captivity by paying a ransom: "As the mighty Word, and very man, who, redeeming us by His own blood in a manner consonant to reason, gave Himself as a redemption for those who had been led into captivity . . . Since the Lord thus has redeemed us through His own blood, giving His soul for our souls, and His flesh for our flesh, and has also poured out the Spirit of the Father for the union and communion of God and man, imparting indeed God to men by means of the Spirit."[1] Irenaeus argued that God purchased us back by exchanging his soul for our souls and his body for our bodies. His term "redemption" is translated as "ransom" in other versions. In this quote, he does not directly mention to whom God paid ransom. But he previously mentioned that we belonged to Satan after the fall: "For at the first Adam became a vessel in his (Satan's) possession, whom he did also hold under his power, that is, by bringing sin on him iniquitously, and under color of immortality entailing death upon him."[2] Adam's fall made all of us captives of Satan, and Jesus gave himself as our ransom to free us.

Tertullian (c. 160–c. 225 CE) is another apologist who elaborated on the metaphor of ransom. To him, Jesus is our ransom releasing us from hell, the principalities that rule the world, the wicked spirits, and eternal judgment and death: "The everlasting gates were lifted up, that the King of Glory, the Lord of might, might enter in, after having redeemed man from earth, nay, from hell, that he might attain to heaven. . . . And the Lord indeed ransomed him from the angelic powers which rule the world—from the spirits of wickedness, from the darkness of this life, from eternal judgment, from everlasting death."[3]

He interchangeably used the terms *deliver* and *ransom*. He held that the precious blood of Jesus ransomed and redeemed people from the angelic powers, the spirit of wickedness, and the darkness of life, but he did not specify who received the ransom. Here the ransom is not a literal ransom, but a metaphoric one.

Tertullian furthermore made his point that we use our liberty for Christ after being ransomed: "But you have been already ransomed by Christ, and that at a great price. How shall the world manumit the servant of another? Though it seems to be liberty, yet it will come to be found bondage. . . . For even then, as ransomed by Christ, you were under no bondage to man; and now, though man has given you liberty, you are the servant of Christ."[4] We are no one's slave, but only Christ's.

Origen (c. 182/185–c. 251/254 CE) was one of the most creative Christian thinkers to use the idea of ransom for the description of Christ's redemption. While we were the prisoners of our enemies, Jesus, with his human nature, freed us from their power because of his sinlessness: "But Christ is our redemption because we had become prisoners and needed ransoming. I do not enquire as to His own redemption, for though He was tempted in all things as we are, He was without sin, and His enemies never reduced Him to captivity."[5]

Christ is the wisdom and power of God that delivers us from our enemies. Human beings had no power to break off the chains of the prison, and Jesus came to exchange his life for our lives:

> But, if spoken affirmatively, I think, to indicate that there is not anything in man by the giving of which in exchange for his own life which has been overcome by death, he will ransom it out of its hand. A man, therefore, could not give anything as an exchange for his own life, but God gave an exchange for the life of us all, "the precious blood of Christ Jesus," according as "we were bought with a price," "having been redeemed, not with corruptible things as silver or gold, but with precious blood, as of a lamb without blemish and without spot," even of Christ.[6]

God purchased us with the priceless blood of the Lamb. God ransomed the helpless human beings not with gold or silver but with Jesus' incorruptible blood. Origen also held that Jesus' death began to break the dominion of the devil over the world so that hostages could escape from their bondage: "His death being not only an example of death endured for the sake of piety, but also the first blow in the conflict which is to overthrow the power of that evil spirit the devil, who had obtained dominion over the whole world. For we have signs and pledges of the destructions of his empire, in those who through the coming of Christ are everywhere escaping from the power of demons."[7] The evil kingdom began to fall, and the delivered started to devote themselves to the advancement of God's reign.

Gregory of Nyssa (c. 335–c. 395) developed a fully fledged theory of ransom. The Deity in sublime power came to exist in lowliness. The Enemy saw in Christ an opportunity for an advance, in the exchange, upon the value of his hostages. For this reason the Enemy selected Christ as a ransom for those who were shut up in the prison of death. The Enemy must have seen in him some portion of the fleshly nature of the sinful humanity held in his bondage. Therefore, the Enemy accepted Christ, the Deity invested with the flesh, as a ransom, not knowing the hidden deity under the veil of his humanity. Like a voracious fish, the Enemy swallowed up the hook, the bait of Christ's flesh, not realizing that darkness cannot conquer light. By engulfing the source of life, the power of the death of the Enemy was destroyed.

> For since, as has been said before, it was not in the nature of the opposing power to come in contact with the undiluted presence of God, and to undergo His unclouded manifestation, therefore, in order to secure that the ransom in our behalf might be easily accepted by him who required it, the Deity was hidden under the veil of our nature, that so, as with ravenous fish, the hook of the Deity might be gulped down along with the bait of flesh, and thus, life being introduced into the house of death, and light shining in darkness, that which is diametrically opposed to light and life might vanish.[8]

This metaphor pictures God as a fisher hooking the devil with the bait of Jesus' human body. The devil's power of death was destroyed by Christ's divinity, and we were saved by life. The lack of life makes death active, and the life of Christ defeated the death power of the devil.

Augustine (354–430) further explained the ransom idea with a well-known metaphor of the trap. Adam was seduced and held captive by Satan. Jesus came to release humanity from Satan's grip by trapping Satan. His blood was bait for Satan:

> For we fell into the hands of the prince of this world, who seduced Adam, and made him his servant, and began to possess us as his slaves. But the Redeemer came, and the seducer was overcome. And what did our Redeemer to him who held us captive? For our ransom he held out His Cross as a trap; he placed in It as a bait His Blood. He indeed had power to shed His Blood, he did not attain to drink it. And in that he shed the Blood of Him who was no debtor, he was commanded to render up the debtors; he shed the Blood of the Innocent, he was commanded to withdraw from the guilty. He verily shed His Blood to this end, that He might wipe out our sins.[9]

God is a trapper as well as a judge in this metaphor. Jesus' blood was the ransom as well as the bait and cleared the debt of our sins. This is a dramatic metaphor to describe the work of Jesus' redemption in a double story. God trapped the devil, using Jesus' blood as the bait, and ordered him to leave sinful humanity alone because the devil had shed the blood of an innocent.

The ransom theory has its strengths. First, some biblical passages support the idea of ransom (Mark 10:45; Matt. 20:28; 1 Cor. 6:20; 7:23; 1 Tim. 2:6; 2 Pet. 2:1) in which Jesus purchased us with his own blood. Second, the ransom theory addresses the reality of the power of evil over us. We are not free but in bondage. Third, it stresses the importance of the integration of Jesus' death and resurrection for his work of salvation. It highlights the decisiveness of the resurrection of Jesus in his redemptive work.

However, this theory also has several weaknesses. First, some theologians have developed the biblical idea of ransom too literally. It is metaphoric, not actual. Thus, this theory paints God as a trickster and Satan as a naive, unintelligent being. Second, human beings committed sins against God, not against Satan. Thus, there was no reason why Satan would have held humanity to ransom. Third, if Jesus purchased us back from Satan, all human beings are supposed to be free in daily life. We are not.

The Christus Victor Theory

This view depicts Christ as the military leader of a fight against the evil enemy of God. Christ defeats the power of darkness and death to free us from its domain. It has biblical foundations, such as Ephesians 6:12 (spiritual warfare), Revelation 12:7–17 (Michael and his angels against the dragon). Christ's blood has the power to conquer the power of Satan. This view is represented by the following hymns:

> Stand up, stand up for Jesus, ye soldiers of the cross;
> Lift high His royal banner, it must not suffer loss.
> From victory unto victory His army shall He lead,
> Till every foe is vanquished, and Christ is Lord indeed.
> (G. Duffield 1858)

> Onward, Christian soldiers, marching as to war,
> With the cross of Jesus going on before.
> Christ, the royal Master, leads against the foe;
> Forward into battle see his banners go!
> (S. B. Gould 1864)

> A mighty fortress is our God, a bulwark never failing;
> Our helper He, amid the flood of mortal ills prevailing:
> For still our ancient foe doth seek to work us woe;
> His craft and power are great, and, armed with cruel hate,
> On earth is not his equal.
> (M. Luther 1529)

As we see in these popular hymns, Christ is depicted as the Royal Conqueror in the cosmic battle with Satan, leading the host of his people into the midst of the battle.

Early church thinkers supported this picture of Christ as victor. Justin Martyr (c. 100–c. 165 CE) said that Christ defeated death by suffering, dying, and rising again: "He endured both to be set at nought and to suffer, that by dying and rising again He might conquer death."[10] Furthermore, Jesus came to overthrow the serpent and its work: "And by her [Mary] has He been born, to whom we have proved so many Scriptures refer, and by whom God destroys both the serpent and those angels and men who are like him."[11] Justin depicted Jesus as the slayer of the serpent and his followers.

To Irenaeus, after creation, Satan defeated God's purpose by persuading human beings to betray God and to fasten themselves to him, but through the incarnation, Christ defeated and bound Satan just as Satan had bound human beings, setting human beings free from the power of sin:

> For as in the beginning he enticed man to transgress his Maker's law, and thereby got him into his power; yet his power consists in transgression and apostasy, and with these he bound man [to himself]; so again, on the other hand, it was necessary that through man himself he should, when conquered, be bound with the same chains with which he had bound man, in order that man, being set free, might return to his Lord, leaving to him [Satan] those bonds by which he himself had been fettered, that is, sin. For when Satan is bound, man is set free.[12]

Irenaeus drew the image of Christ as the conqueror who bound and chained Satan. He upheld the view that Jesus is the beginning of re-creation by reforming human nature and conquering Satan: "As I have pointed out in the preceding book, the apostle did, in the first place, instruct the Gentiles . . . that His Son was His Word, by whom He founded all things; and that He, in the last times, was made a man among men; that He reformed the human race, but destroyed and conquered the enemy of man, and gave to His handiwork victory against the adversary."[13] Christ is the Word of God in the flesh that creates new things and new beings and destroys the adversary to God's

creation. With his authentic human nature, Christ defeated
Satan by exposing his identity so that Satan would be subjugated to human beings: "The Word of God, however, the
Maker of all things, conquering him by means of human
nature, and showing him to be an apostate, has, on the contrary, put him under the power of man."[14] Christ conquered
Satan through his manifestation of God's new humanity.

By publishing *Christus Victor*, Gustaf Aulén (1879–1977)
shared his theological conviction that this dramatic view of
atonement is authentically biblical. It focuses on the divine conflict and victory. Christ battles and "triumphs over the evil
power of the world, the 'tyrants' under which mankind is in
bondage and suffering, and in Him God reconciles the world to
Himself."[15] He believed that this idea was upheld by the New
Testament and the early church. Consequently, he called it "the
classic idea of the Atonement." Aulén points out some unsatis-
factory aspects of Anselm's satisfaction theory and Peter
Abelard's moral influence theory. Based on the forensic idea of
sin and the objective sense of justice, Anselm's theory regards
atonement as human work of Jesus Christ for human sin, not as
God's work for humanity. While the classic idea of atonement is
"a *continuous* Divine work," Anselm's satisfaction theory is "a
discontinuous Divine work."[16] Focusing on the subjective change
of human hearts, Abelard's atonement theory neglects "a complete change in the situation, a change in the relation between
God and the world, and a change also in God's own attitude."[17]

Because of the two traditional accounts of atonement theories, the objective view of Anselm's satisfaction theory and the
subjective view of Abelard's moral influence theory, the classic
idea had been overlooked for a long time. Aulén sums up this
idea in two phrases: "Christus Victor" and "God's reconciling
with the world in Christ." He connects the incarnation with
the atonement, proclaiming that God in Christ delivers us
from the power of evil.[18] He asserted that this classic idea was
reinvigorated by Luther. Under the name of the "classic idea,"
he includes the model of dualistic battles between God and
Satan and the model of ransom.

Aulén finds in the Pauline epistles all the traits of the classic view of the atonement; Christ came to set the human race free from sin, death, and the law. Paul affirmed that Christ prevailed over the array of hostile forces such as "principalities," "powers," "thrones," and "dominions" (Eph. 6:12).[19] The Synoptic Gospels with other New Testament books stress the image of ransom (Mark 10:45; Eph. 1:7; 1 Tim. 2:6; Rev. 1:5). The Johannine writings and the book of Revelation consider the world standing against God as a dark, hostile power, showing their dualistic view: light over darkness, life over death, and good over evil. To the end was the Son of God revealed that he might crush the works of the devil (1 John 3:8). To Aulén, the Pauline epistles and other New Testament books embrace the double-sidedness of the classic idea: Christ as Victor and God in Christ reconciling with the world.

In Aulén's view, Irenaeus articulated the classic idea by lifting up the work of Christ that delivered human hostages from the enemies that held them in the bondage of sin and death. Sin is a state of separation from God and spiritual death. The devil is a usurper, and Christ brings forth God's redemption to restore God's original creation—the recapitulation (*apocatasis*). Christ's incarnation, his obedient life, his death and resurrection, and the coming of the Holy Spirit work to fulfill the redemption of God.

To Aulén, Luther's teaching was confused with the Latin type of atonement (satisfaction theory) because he used such terms as *merit* and *satisfaction*. Aulén contends that Luther spoke very negatively about the satisfaction theory of the atonement.[20] Instead of the satisfaction theory, Luther revived the classic idea of atonement by stressing three points. First, God's omnipotence is able to overcome the tyrants that include "law" and "the wrath of God." Both of these tyrants exhibit the double-sidedness of the classic idea. Second, God who is in Christ overcomes the tyrants. Third, in a tremendous conflict of duality, Christ prevails. Listening to Luther's hymns makes us feel the thrills of triumph in the midst of struggle.

Aulén's view on the classic idea has been well respected. His idea realistically reminds us of our daily struggle with the power of injustice and evil. Early church thinkers as well affirmed that Christ defeated principalities and the powers of darkness for us.

Aulén's critics, however, believe that he overemphasizes the importance of the classic idea for early church thinkers. Lutheran theologian Ted Peters comments that Aulén's assessment on Luther's rejection of the satisfaction theory is wrong. Even though Luther used the imagery of Christ as victor, he did not exclude the terms *satisfaction, payment,* and *punishment* in depicting the work of Christ. To Peters, the satisfaction theory underpins Luther's notion of justification by faith.[21] Furthermore, Peters rightly evaluates Aulén's classic idea as excluding the atoning work of Jesus Christ as a full human.[22]

My uneasiness with Aulén's view is due to the mixture of Christ as victor with a ransom theory. The ransom theory focuses on the blood of Jesus paying to release the human race from Satan, who is a counterpart of negotiation, while the idea of Christ as victor is about conquering Satan and his forces. In terms of a dualistic struggle, these two are similar, but their ways of dealing with Satan are different. The ransom theory treats Satan as a legitimate opponent of negotiation, while the idea of Christ as victor views Satan as the enemy to be defeated.

There are additional shortcomings of Aulén's Christus Victor view. First, this theory says that Satan is defeated by Jesus, but the defeated Satan wields too much power in the present world. If Christ rules in the world, why do we not experience permanent peace? Second, this theory does not involve human beings in the drama of salvation. We are just passive observers, not participants in the history of salvation. It is too celestial and not terrestrial enough. Third, it blames Satan for all the problems and sins in the world. Aren't human beings responsible for the injustice, violence, and evil of the world? Fourth, it suggests that all human beings are freed from Satan's bondage by Christ's victory. Consequently, Christ's victory warrants the salvation of humanity. In reality, Christ's victory over Satan, however, has not brought salvation to all sinners. Fifth, it does not differentiate sinners (oppressors) from the sinned-against (the oppressed) in the process of salvation. This theory overlooks the fact that the reconciliation between the oppressors and the oppressed is a significant part of Christian salvation.

The Christus Victor theory has its strengths too. First, it counts both the death and resurrection of Jesus for our salvation, as does the ransom theory. Second, it acknowledges our struggle against some forces of evil beyond human sins: the rulers, the authorities, and the cosmic powers of this present darkness (Eph. 6:12). Third, it realistically describes our daily struggles with the power of evil.

The Satisfaction Theory

Anselm of Canterbury (1033–1109) grapples with the issue of the incarnation and the death of Jesus for the restoration of the world in his book *Cur Deus Homo* (Why God Became a Human Being). Criticizing the ransom theory, he adamantly declares that the devil has no just claim against human beings. Since God is all-powerful, it is not necessary to negotiate with the devil for the release of the human race. The issue is between God and human beings, not between God and the devil. God can save human beings by God's own will.

Is it fair, however, to forgive sin simply out of mercy alone, apart from any restoration of divine justice? Anselm is strongly opposed to the idea that sinners who defiled the honor of God repay nothing for their wrongs. Human beings must restore God's honor by satisfying God's justice; they cannot be saved without taking responsibility for how they have dishonored God.

Sin, being against the infinite God, is infinitely guilty and can be atoned for only by an infinite satisfaction. Sin against the infinite God is infinitely grave, and no finite being including angels can atone for it. Someone needs to pay to God for the sin of the human race "something greater than every existing thing besides God."[23] Since in feudal society the offense of a person must be recompensed by a person of an equal status, a human being that represents the human race yet is equal to God is necessary. Since nothing is greater than God, it is only God who can restore God's honor: "Whoever can give to God something of his own which surpasses everything that is less than God must be greater than everything that is not God. . . . Therefore, only God can make this satisfaction. . . . But only a man ought to make this satisfaction. For in any other case it would not be man who makes it."[24] Since only a human being ought to make satisfaction and only God is able to do the job, it was necessary to have a God-human reconcile God and human beings. This is the reason why God assumed a human nature from the race of Adam and from a virgin.

Jesus was fully divine and fully human. He let himself be killed for the sake of the justice of paying back to God. His death was the act to restore the honor of God.[25] His death was also an example of justice for humanity: "Do you not realize that when He endured with patient kindness the injuries, the abuses, the crucifixion among thieves—which were all inflicted upon Him (as I said above) for the sake of the justice which He obediently kept—He gave men an example, in order that they would not, on account of any detriments they can experience, turn aside from the justice they owe to God?"[26] The human race owed a debt to God, and Jesus paid it off. Jesus is part of the Trinity, yet he restored the honor of the Trinity:

> Surely, that honor belongs to the whole Trinity. Therefore, since He Himself is God—viz., the Son of God—He offered Himself to Himself (just as to the Father and the Holy Spirit) for His own honor. That is, [He offered] His humanity to His divinity, which is one and the same divinity common to the three persons. . . . For in this way we speak most fittingly. For by reference to one person [viz., the Father] we understand it to be God as a whole to whom the Son offered Himself according to His humanity; and through the name "Father" and the name "Son," an enormous devotion is felt in the hearts of those listening when the Son is said to entreat the Father for us in this way.[27]

Jesus' humanity was offered to his divinity inseparable from the triune God. On our behalf, Jesus pleaded with God by offering himself. God's honor was restored in justice through Christ's death.

This atonement idea has its strength as well as some problems. Its strength is to deliver the church from the ransom the-

ory. God does not transact with Satan to save humanity.
Anselm intended to develop the atonement idea that involves
humanity, not Satan. He did not, however, succeed. His shortcomings are several. First, in order to forgive sinful humanity,
does God demand the satisfactory payment from them on the
basis of God's justice? If so, God's justice is retributive rather
than restorative or gracious. Second, his satisfaction theory
does not involve human beings except for the humanity of
Jesus. It is a transaction between God and Jesus. There is no
involvement of human actions in his theory. Third, he totally
ignores the presence of the power of Satan in the drama of
Jesus' salvation. Since Jesus dealt with God, the power of evil
was unreal in God's world. Fourth, if God was satisfied and forgave human sins because of Jesus' death, have people after
Jesus' death been free from sin? Did Jesus die for the sins of all
his contemporaries? Did he die for all the generations before
him too? Does Jesus' blood satisfy future sins of humanity? If it
does, all human beings are totally free from sin and are saved.
If it does not, we need another God-human. Fifth, this satisfaction theory ignores the meaning of the resurrection for our
salvation. Anselm needs to make a clear connection between
the crucifixion and the resurrection in terms of God's salvific
plan. Sixth, his understanding of Christ's nature is problem-
atic. Jesus' humanity is inseparable from his divinity. Thus, it is
absurd that Jesus offered his humanity to his divinity in the
Trinitarian context.

The Moral Influence Theory

Clement understood that Christ's blood was poured out to save us through the grace of repentance. The way the blood of Christ saves us is not through magic, but through the indispensable process of repentance:

> Let us look steadfastly to the blood of Christ, and see how precious that blood is to God, which, having been shed for our salvation, has·set the grace of repentance before the whole world. Let us turn to every age that has passed, and learn that, from generation to generation, the Lord has granted a place of repentance to all such as would be converted unto Him.[28]

Clement further says that Christ endured and suffered the cross on account of us. To him, Christ's blood alone cannot save us without our repentance. The precious blood graces us with repentance. By emphasizing Christ's work for our repentance, he underpins the moral influence theory.

Peter Abelard (1079–1142) represents the extension of this theme in the medieval moral influence theory. His view starts with his understanding of sin as the "contempt of God or consent to evil."[29] Since little children and the mentally challenged are immune from such a sin, Abelard denies original sin. He rejects the idea that Jesus' death was for the forgiveness of our original sin or actual sins. God forgives our sins without the blood of Jesus: "Indeed, how cruel and wicked it seems that anyone should demand the blood of an innocent person as the price for anything, or that it should in any way please him that an innocent man should be slain—still less that God should consider the death of his Son so agreeable that by it he should be reconciled to the whole world!"[30]

In his *Exposition of the Epistle to the Romans*, Abelard explains his position on the atonement. He raises questions about the meaning of the death of Christ for our atonement. Since the time of the primitive church, no formal doctrine of the atonement has been instituted, and the devil has played an important role in the atonement of humanity because the devil has been thought to have obtained some kind of right over sinful human beings. In the ransom theory, when the devil attempted to gain the upper hand over Jesus, he was conquered. To Abelard, Christ did not incarnate to deliver human beings from the bondage of the devil. Before Abelard, Anselm of Canterbury opposed this strange ransom theory and developed a new doctrine of atonement, the so-called satisfaction theory.[31]

Concurring with Anselm, Abelard criticized the traditional doctrine of the devil's right as absurd. To him, it would be much easier for God to forgive sinners than deal with the devil. The question then persists: if God can forgive sinners, why did the Son of God suffer and die for them? Can it be that the death of the innocent Jesus pleased God so much that God reconciled with sinful humanity? Can the death of Jesus make us more just than we were before his death? Anselm interpreted the death of Jesus as the full satisfaction to God, but Abelard, unaffected by Anselm's idea, saw it as the expression of God's love that teaches us by the word and example of Jesus. Abelard found the revelation of God's deep love in the suffering of Christ. He understood Jesus as our exemplar and the cross as the expression of God's love for us. Abelard stressed that it is Christ's love expressed in his suffering that frees us from the power of sin and ensures us the freedom of God's children. God does not save us in fear but in love. The following is the core of his theory of the work of Christ:

> We believe that none the less we are justified in the blood of Christ, and reconciled to God by the singular grace shown

unto us whereby His Son took upon Him our nature, and in it taught us by word and by example and so endured unto death, and thus drew us closer to Himself by love: so that fired by so great a benefit of divine grace true love should not be afraid to endure anything for His sake. This benefit indeed we do not doubt kindled the early Fathers also (who looked forward to it by faith) into the highest love for God, no less than the men in these years of grace. . . . Therefore our redemption is that supreme love which exists in us through the passion of Christ, which not only frees us from the servitude of sin, but wins for us the true liberty of the children of God, so that we fulfill all things by love of Him rather than by fear of Him, who showed us such grace that cannot be excelled, as He Himself bore witness, saying, "Greater love hath no man than this, that a man should lay down his life for his friends."[32]

For Abelard, we are justified in the blood of Jesus by his grace. The suffering of Christ redeems us through arousing our deeper love that not only delivers us from slavery to sin but also acquires for us our true status as children of God. The blood of Jesus saves us by moving us to repentance.

In addition, Abelard assesses Jesus' whole life as his work. He was not born just to bear the cross. He lived and died to show his love and draw us to love him back. By loving him, we are saved from sin. Loving him means to have the mind of Christ in us.[33]

Abelard has an alternative theology of the work of Christ:

When God made his Son man he straightway made him under the law which He had given in common to all men, and so by divine precept that Man needs must love His neighbour as Himself and show His love to us by teaching us and by praying for us. . . . Thus it is laid upon Him by His love for His neighbour that he might redeem those that were under the law, and could not be saved by the law, and that His merits might supply what was lacking in ours; and as He was unique in holiness so He should be unique in the services rendered to others in working their salvation.[34]

Abelard stressed our loving life in Jesus as a way to salvation. The law does not save us, but loving our neighbor does. Christ's merit of love on the cross provides us the holiness of salvation. Abelard's theological ethic is the core of his understanding of salvation: the transcendent saving love of God is what necessitates the crucifixion of Jesus.

The cross reveals God's love that spurs our responsive love. Abelard mentioned few benefits of Christ's redeeming work except that it revealed the love of God, but he stressed the importance of repentance in salvation: "Therefore, wherever there is true repentance coming only from God's love, no contempt of God remains, especially since Truth says: 'If anyone loves me, he will keep my word. And my Father will love him; and we will come to him and will make our abode with him.' So whoever persists in the love of God must be saved. This salvation would by no means happen if one sin, that is, one contempt of God remains."[35] The cross stirs up the deepest love of God within us, releasing us from the power of sin and empowering us to repent of our sins.

The cross has the power to move us to bear the cross with Christ. In the cross we become true and we carry his shame and blame upon us. The moral influence theory focuses on the cross of Jesus Christ that inspires us to turn around from our sins and follow him in love.

This moral influence theory has its strengths. First, it stresses a love of God that is biblical and essential to Christianity. Jesus' atonement is about God's love, not about God's business deal with the devil. Second, it involves repentance for salvation, requiring human participation in and responses to God's action. Christ's work is not to appease God, but to transform human hearts. Third, it counts Jesus' exemplary life for the work of salvation and exhorts us to follow Jesus, not just to worship him. Fourth, it emphasizes the importance of Jesus' whole life, while the satisfaction theory focuses on his death.

This moral influence theory has its shortcomings too. First, it holds that Jesus died on the cross to show God's love for us. Jesus was not killed, however, to show God's love on the cross.

Jesus came to proclaim and establish God's reign. Jesus' mission statement (Luke 4:18–21) precludes his death as his primary goal. God did not send Jesus to die on the cross to show God's love for sinners. Denny Weaver points out that it was not God who let Jesus be killed, but the power of evil that killed Jesus.[36] Second, it underestimates the reality of the power of evil in the world in reaction to the ransom theory. To Abelard, the devil only follows God's will.[37] He overlooked the reality of evil in our daily life. Third, it overlooks the meaning of the resurrection for our salvation, while stressing the influence of Jesus' death over our change of hearts. Abelard needed to articulate the integral meaning of the crucifixion and the resurrection for our salvation. Fourth, this theory disregards Jesus' work for the sinned-against. Does Jesus' crucifixion influence the victims of sin only to repent of their own sins? God cares about the healing of the wounded.

The Penal Substitution Theory

Anselm's satisfaction theory was further developed during the Reformation era. Trained as a lawyer, Calvin significantly modified it by interpreting Christ's death as a penalty paid to God. God's justice demands the expiation of sinners. God cannot let the sin of the human race go without penalty.

Calvin considers the death of Jesus not as a satisfaction to God but as a substitute for our punishment: "That then Christ interposed, took the punishment upon himself and bore what by the just judgment of God was impending over sinners."[38] Christ substituted himself to pay the price of our redemption. He transferred our punishment to himself. His way of death on the cross indicates his voluntary submission to the curse, the punishment of sins.

Before our reconciliation with God through Christ, we were God's enemies, deserving God's wrath, vengeance, and eternal death. A perfectly just God could not love our iniquities. God's love, however, urged God to receive us into God's favor. That action of God's love was the atonement of Christ.

Through his obedience, Christ accomplished his atonement for us. His obedience was his voluntary subjection to God's will. He was condemned to death as an evildoer. His suffering was real and awful because he assumed our infirmities. He struggled with condemnation and death.

The punishment Christ took upon himself includes the agony of his soul through which he completed the substitution of our spiritual and physical punishment: "And certainly had not his soul shared in the punishment, he would have been a Redeemer of bodies only."[39] He descended into hell to feel the full extension of divine vengeance, undergoing the horrors of eternal death. His cry, "My God, my God, why have you for-saken me?" reveals his utter anguish, bearing the tortures of the condemned in his soul.

Although Calvin uses the term *substitute*, he employs more than one expression to describe Christ's atonement. Christ's death is not only a substitute for us, but also for ransom and propitiation: Christ is "our substitute—ransom and propitia-tion."[40] In the ransom theory, God paid the ransom to the devil. In contrast, for Calvin, Christ paid our ransom to death because it took us hostage: "Death held us under its yoke, but he in our place delivered himself into its power, that he might exempt us from it."[41] To satisfy our ransom, Christ gave him-self up to the condemnation of death.

Another expression Calvin uses for the atonement is *propiti-ation*. Christ's blood expiates our sins and propitiates God's anger: "with his own blood expiated the sins which rendered them hateful to God, by this expiation satisfied and duly propi-tiated God the Father, by this intercession appeased his anger, on this basis founded peace between God and men, and by this tie secured the Divine benevolence toward them."[42] Calvin believes that God was not hostile toward us before the death of Jesus; instead, God loved us even before the propitiation of his death (John 3:16). His death abolishes all the evil that is in us so that we may be clean and new. Calvin freely uses such terms as *substitution*, *satisfaction*, *ransom*, *expiation*, and *propitiation* to explain the powerful work of Christ for our atonement. The idea of substitution runs through his atonement theology: "Here again it is necessary to consider how he substituted him-self in order to pay the price of our redemption."[43] Concretely, Jesus' blood acts as "the laver to purge our defilements."[44]

Furthermore, the resurrection of Christ is the capstone of his atonement for us. Without the resurrection, his death ends up with despondence. It is Christ's resurrection that provides us the hope of eternal life: "Hence, although in his death we have an effectual completion of salvation, because by it we are reconciled to God, satisfaction is given to his justice, the curse is removed, and the penalty paid; still it is not by his death, but by his resurrection, that we are said to be begotten again to a living hope (1 Pet. 1:3) because, as he, by rising again, became victorious over death, so the victory of our faith consists only in his resurrection."[45] His resurrection brings the restoration to God's life and power in us. His resurrection empowers the works of his death by offering our victory over the power of death. Calvin makes use of the idea of Christus Victor to legitimate his penal substitution theory after all.

This penal substitution theory has its strength. First, it is supported by several biblical passages: 2 Corinthians 5:21 ("For our sake he made him to be sin who knew no sin, so that in him we might become the righteousness of God"), Galatians 3:13 ("Christ redeemed us from the curse of the law by becoming a curse for us—for it is written, 'Cursed is everyone who hangs on a tree'"), Hebrews 9:22 ("Indeed, under the law almost everything is purified with blood, and without the shedding of blood there is no forgiveness of sins"), and Romans 6:23 ("For the wages of sin is death"). Its problem is the literal interpretation and application of these passages to our salvation. Second, in this theory we find the effort to integrate the meaning of Jesus' death and resurrection for our salvation.

But this theory also has several weaknesses. First, it promotes violence in the name of salvation. The God we believe in does not promote any violence through the punishment of a person by death. Recently, feminist and womanist theologians have rejected the satisfaction theory and the penal substitution theory as promoting child abuse. The idea that God "the Father" punishes "his Son" for saving others may justify child abuse in society. The redemptive side of suffering may promote the suffering of wives in the family. For Rosemary Ruether, suffering is not redemptive but is the result of confrontation with evil— "the risk that one takes when one struggles to overcome unjust systems whose beneficiaries resist change."[46] Notably, Rita Brock, Joanne Brown, and Rebecca Parker have rejected the violent dimensions of several atonement theories. For example, Brock says, "Such doctrines of salvation reflect by analogy, I believe, images of the neglect of children or, even worse, child abuse, making it acceptable as divine behavior-cosmic child abuse, as it were."[47] Womanist theologian Delores Williams criticizes the substitution theory as the image of divine surrogacy: "Redemption of humans can have nothing to do with any kind of surrogate or substitute role Jesus was reputed to have played in a bloody act that supposedly gained victory over sin and/or evil."[48] Second, the penal substitution theory erases the picture of the forgiveness of God that is the essential teaching of Jesus. Can't God forgive sinners without punishing them or their substitute? The entire concept of substitutionary punishment is incongruent with the God of forgiveness that Jesus taught. Third, this theory assumes the transferability of our portion of punishment to Jesus. It is unjust to punish an innocent person for the sins of others.

As in the satisfaction theory, the penal substitution theory also lacks human involvement in Jesus' redemptive drama, overlooks a clear connection between the crucifixion and the resurrection in God's plan for human salvation, and supports the unlimited permission to sin for all the people after Jesus' death.

The Last Scapegoat Theory

Christian anthropologist René Girard (b. 1923) developed a theory of mimetic violence and has interpreted Jesus' death from that perspective. He traced back to the origin of violence in archaic religion. He found human behavior fundamentally mimetic. Human beings tend to copy each other's behavior. This mimesis does not have to generate conflict among us, but in actuality it spawns the conflict of rivalry. In a playground, when two children play with toys, they tend to fight over one particular toy, leaving all other toys behind. Adults may continue such mimetic rivalry in competitive forms of relationships. As mimetic rivalry grows intense, it is likely that more people will join in. Such conflict may heighten the tension, conflict, and violence of society, whose very survival may hang in the balance.

In a primitive society, as the tension of mimetic rivalry reaches the brink of self-destruction, the society suddenly directs its attention to one person. This person is supposed to be liable for all of the social conflict and uproar. Such an ideal victim must be a member of the community but be marginalized enough to avert the eruption of uproar or revenge.

The community exterminates the marked person through impulsive mob violence. The sacrifice of such a victim reinstates the peace and order of the community drastically. Girard calls this process a scapegoating mechanism. To Girard, scapegoating produces rituals of sacrifice to alleviate the social and cultural pressure of violence. The social escalation of mimetic conflict itself prompts the scapegoating mechanism of collective violence, generating the camaraderie of the community. Sacrificial ritual and myth sustain such communal camaraderie.

Girard understands the meaning of Jesus' death in this light. The critical difference between the story of the Gospels and other archaic religious myths is that the Christ event tries to end the ritual of the sacrifice of a scapegoat: "In the first period after my conversion to Christianity in 1959 I was convinced of the strict opposition between archaic religions and Christianity. I held this position because I saw archaic religions as sacrificial and Christianity as strongly antisacrificial. It seemed clear to me that archaic religions continue the pattern of scapegoating, and Christianity seeks to bring it to an end."[49]

Girard acknowledges that symbolism in archaic religion shares a common ground with Christianity. For example, the Eucharist uses the same symbol of cannibalism, of eating the flesh and drinking the blood. But if we look closely, we will see that the symbolism of Eucharist in Christianity brings the esoteric sacrificial pattern of archaic religions into the open square to disintegrate its dark side: "The Eucharist can be a link to primal religions because it includes within itself the same symbolism of eating a body and drinking blood, but it reverses the point of view of sacrificial myths."[50] While archaic religions feed on the scapegoat resolution of mimetic crises, lynching and devouring the victim of communal violence, Christianity reverses the resolution by presenting the death of an innocent scapegoat that openly defies the unjust treatment of a victim and the belief of the crowd. In Oedipus and other myths, heroes and heroines are truly guilty for the crimes of which they are accused, but in the Gospels, Jesus is the innocent victim whose purpose of suffering is to end such a sacrificial mechanism for the violence of a mimetic contagion.

Girard believes that the cross of Christ leads the truth to victory. Jesus' crucifixion is a scapegoating mechanism. His cross restores all the victims of the scapegoating mechanism whether it goes under the label of legal accusation, Satan, or principalities and powers.[51] Satan obliged humans to be indebted to him and made them coconspirators with him in crimes. The cross of Jesus seemed to comply with the game rule of Satan's violence but in reality revealed Satan's crime of violence and slavery and liberated humans from Satan's bondage.[52] By crucifying Jesus, the powers assumed that they put him under the scapegoat victim mechanism. Christ's victory is different from that of military generals. They underestimated the revelatory power of the cross.[53] He obtained his victory by submitting to the satanic violence and revealed what it tried to hide. His passion was an antisacrificial ritual of victimization. He was the last scapegoat of violence. Before the resurrection of Jesus, no power could match the power of mimetic unanimity. Jesus' resurrection changed this. The resurrection was not only "a miracle, a prodigious transgression of natural laws," but it was also "the spectacular sign of the entrance into the world of a power superior to violent contagion."[54]

In his system, the Paraclete plays a very significant role. The Paraclete is "lawyer for the defense" or "defender of the accused." To Girard, Christianity was born in the victory of the Paraclete over Satan, the accuser against victims.

Girard's scapegoat theory supports the Christus Victor view. He thinks that the Greek fathers rightly depicted Satan as being "caught in the trap of his own mystification" by the cross.[55] God did not trick him. Satan himself converted his own mechanism into a trap, and he foolishly stepped into it. To Girard, Satan is the mimetic cycle, the violence itself. Christ's passion broke the power of mimetic unanimity and the single victim mechanism, and the Paraclete defends Satan's victims.

The revelation of the Bible centers on the fact that God sides with the victims. Instead of demanding victims, God identifies with the victims in Jesus and dismantles the surrogate victim mechanism. For a long period, "Christianity has done nothing to 'resolve the problem of violence,'" perpetuating the vicious cycle of scapegoating others.[56] The message of the Gospels dismantles the mythological scapegoating mechanism. God incarnates in history as Jesus, who goes to his death as the scapegoat. God counterbalances our violence with nonviolent love. For Girard, God's solidarity with the victim is the core of the message of the Gospels. To Girard, the church has ignored this central message of God's revelation in Jesus and has misconstrued

Jesus' death as a sacrificial offering to God, who demands victims. Fortunately, modern liberation movements have advocated on behalf of the marginalized, returning Christianity to its essential role of siding with victims, not conquerors.[57] Girard's last scapegoat view strongly urges us to renounce the violence of scapegoating and instead to choose a nonviolent future for humanity.

His last scapegoat theory has several strong points. First, he points out that human violence killed Jesus. Neither God's wrath nor God's voluntary decision caused Jesus' death. Second, he understands religions and their rituals as efforts to reduce conflict and violence and to restore order and calm in society. Third, he highlights Jesus as the last scapegoat, resonating with the biblical imagery of Jesus as the Lamb of God who takes away the sin of the world (John 1:29). Fourth, Girard stresses the importance of the resurrection in the work of God's salvation. Jesus' resurrection is the power superior to satanic contagion.

This theory has its shortcomings. First, Girard diagnoses conflict, rivalry, and violence as the foundation of human nature, culture, and civilization. He has laid little foundation to verify his claims, however, except providing some historical incidents and particular stories. Second, the last scapegoat theory has not been proven in history. The vicious cycle of injustice and violence has been going on after Christ's death as the last scapegoat. We don't see violence in the world subsiding, but rather escalating. In reality, we need to struggle with the power of evil and violence in our daily life. Girard's theory contradicts the reality of life. Third, Girard's theory emphasizes the overcoming of violence. Christ's atoning work is not just to end violence but also to transform human hearts. Our mimetic nature needs to be transformed by Christ's work so that we may truly care for and freely love others.

The Nonviolent Narrative
Christus Victor Theory

Since Anselm developed the satisfaction view in the eleventh century, it has dominated Western churches and their soteriology, along with the sixteenth-century penal substitution theory of the Reformers. A number of black, feminist, and womanist theologians have criticized the satisfaction and penal substitution views because of their amoral and abusive aspects. In *God of the Oppressed,* James Cone particularly points out the lack of ethical dimensions in the satisfaction theory used by white racists.[58] Stimulated by their insights and affirming his Mennonite peace tradition, J. Denny Weaver, a Mennonite theologian, has recently come up with a new nonviolent atonement theology, which he calls a "narrative Christus Victor" view.

His view continues the theme of the classical Christus Victor theory yet is different from it, accentuating Christ's nonviolent triumph over the powers of evil. His view presupposes that "the rejection of violence, whether the direct violence of the sword or the systemic violence of racism or sexism, should be visible in expressions of Christology and atonement."[59] His definition of violence includes "harm or damage," "physical harm or injury to bodily integrity," "damage to person's dignity or self-esteem," or "killing."[60]

Weaver understands Jesus' mission as carrying out God's will "by making the reign of God visible in the world."[61] However, his "mission is so threatening to the world that sinful human beings and the accumulation of evil they represent conspire to kill Jesus."[62] Jesus came to fulfill his mission to witness to God's rule, not to seek his own death. His death was not the will of God but was instigated by the powers that opposed the reign of God.

31

In contrast to the violent retribution of the satisfaction theory, Weaver anchors his narrative Christus Victor to the New Testament—Revelation, the Gospels, Paul, and Hebrews. His Christianity is intrinsically nonviolent. In place of the violence-accommodating theology of Christendom, Weaver suggests a theology that is actually a reading of the Bible's narratives. Such a reading assumes that our Christian identity derives from living within the story of Jesus. To him, Jesus is the norm for ethics. Weaver calls such a reading of the biblical material "a narrative Christology and a narrative Christus Victor for an atonement motif."[63] The narrative theology is a lived theology. Concurring with Karen Baker-Fletcher and Garth Kasimu Baker-Fletcher, who interweave theology and ethics, Weaver's theology is ethics and his ethics is theology.[64]

On the one hand, Revelation, the last book of the New Testament, reveals the multidimensional nature of Christus Victor imagery—"a confrontation between good and evil, between the forces of God and the forces of Satan, between Christ and anti-Christ."[65] The classic imagery of Christus Victor depicts a cosmic battle between the forces of God and the forces of evil. Although the forces of evil hold the souls of humankind as hostages and kill Jesus, the power of God eventually defeats the forces of evil through the resurrection of Jesus, delivering humanity from bondage.

On the other hand, Weaver finds in the Gospels that Jesus challenges "violent or exploitative or oppressive conditions."[66] Some conspicuous events of Jesus' challenge are his healing on the Sabbath as intentional defiance of the prevalent interpretation of the Mosaic law (Luke 6:6–11), his talk with the Samaritan woman as a law-breaking act (John 4:1–30), his other unconventional acts of elevating the status of women (Luke 8:1–3; John 12:1–8), the confrontational act of cleansing the temple (Luke 19:45–46), and the rebuke of Peter's use of a sword at his arrest (Matt. 26:51–54). The way of God's reign in Jesus shows how nonviolently God confronts evil. Jesus' confrontation is nonviolent. God's way of confronting evil shows the nature of God's reign in history.

Weaver developed his theory of narrative Christus Victor to undo Anselm's removal of the "devil" from the story of salvation. He restores the idea of the devil to the salvation equation but reinterprets its image not as that of an individual, personified being, but as that of all structures, institutions, and powers of the world that oppose the rule of God, such as the Roman Empire. Concurring with Walter Wink, he understands the devil as the symbol for all the powers against the reign of God.[67] The "devil" can be us, too.

For Weaver, we play a role in Jesus' death when we side with the powers that killed Jesus. Jesus died for us while we were yet sinners. Weaver envisions the costly forgiveness of God toward sinful humanity. Although "we are all guilty of the killing of Jesus," God forgives us with God's costly grace.[68] In this sense, the death of Jesus was "a vicarious sacrifice 'for us' since Jesus died 'for us' while we were still identified with and in bondage to the powers of death."[69] This vicarious death was not a payment to God, or a punishment by God, but rather the disclosure of the full attributes of the powers against God that enslave sinful humanity: "Through resurrection, God in Christ has in fact defeated these powers 'for us.'"[70] However, until the end, "evil is present but its rule is also limited."[71]

In response to William Placher's penal substitutionary interpretation of the atonement from an oppressor's perspective, Weaver suggests that "a viable theology of atonement should address all people as sinners and speak to the varying conditions in which they find themselves."[72] He believes that narrative Christus Victor speaks to, and for, both the oppressed and the oppressors. By recognizing their oppression, the oppressors can undo their complicity in injustice.

This narrative Christus Victor theory has several strengths. First, Weaver emphasizes the nonviolent resistance of Jesus against injustice and oppression as an important part of his atonement work. Second, he endeavors to include the oppressed and the oppressors in the salvation equation. Third, he integrates his atonement theology with ethics. To tell the story of Jesus is to follow him. Fourth, while several other atonement theories deal exclusively with Jesus' death, his narrative Christus Victor counts Jesus' life, death, and resurrection as significant events for our salvation.

The narrative Christus Victor has its shortcomings also. First, it assumes that Jesus won the victory over the powers of evil through his resurrection, and that evil is present until the eschaton. His narrative theory needs to explain why we have to fight evil until the end if Jesus defeated the powers of evil. Unless Weaver explains more fully why Jesus' rule is limited, the theory seems equivocal. Second, his narrative Christus Victor view emphasizes the resurrection of Jesus as the victory of Christ over the powers of evil. He has not fully recognized the work of the risen Jesus and the Paraclete for the atonement. Third, he equates salvation with liberation in his narrative atonement. Salvation is for the oppressors, while liberation is for the oppressed.

The Symbolic Power of Jesus' Blood

Concerning the blood of Jesus, a number of Christians take this literally in their interpretation. They believe that the "real" blood of Jesus cleanses our sins and saves us. However, many other Christians desire to do away with this idea because of its violent image. We need to differentiate between symbol and sign and to reinterpret the image as a symbol from the perspectives of both the oppressed and the oppressors.

In understanding God's heart, symbols are effective. While a sign is literal, indicating something that represents something else, a symbol is beyond literal, having more than one stratum of meaning. The deeper a symbol is, the greater its strata of meaning.

The term *symbol* does not just mean "figure" but denotes something much more profound. It points to a deeper dimensional reality beyond the plain meaning of language, expressing an ineffable level of reality, yet as Paul Tillich explains, it "participates in that to which it points."[73] It is a conscious and unconscious collective code that sums up universal, cultural, and personal experiences.[74]

Tillich's understanding of sign and symbol is helpful. For him, symbols and signs share the common ground of "pointing beyond themselves to something else."[75] While symbols, however, participate in the reality of that to which they point, signs do not. Thus, symbols are irreplaceable unless there is a historic catastrophe that may change the reality of those symbols, whereas signs are replaceable.[76] Symbols open up dimensions of reality that otherwise are closed for us, and they also unlock concealed depths of our own being. They cannot be artificially invented, but they grow and die as living beings.[77] Human blood functions as both a sign and a symbol. As a sign, it points to the actual fluid consisting of plasma, blood cells, and platelets. As a symbol, it can mean life, family relationships, disposition, temperament, death, passion, or love. Blood has a profound communicative influence.

For the oppressed, Jesus' blood as a symbol participates in the agony of their suffering under unjust persecution, exploitation, oppression, and violence. The blood of Jesus is the violent symbol of human cruelty against fellow humans, particularly against the powerless and the helpless. It symbolizes the many dimensions of the pain of horror, tragedy, injustice, and torment. Pointing to the inhumane violence against the downtrodden, his blood signifies the intermingling of God's woundedness, sorrow, grief, and God's never-ending hope for them. Jesus' blood represents God's pierced heart for the sinned-against.

The symbol of Jesus' blood conjures up a violent and cruel image. This symbol, however, will not die as long as there are victims of violence, cruelty, and injustice. It describes their suffering and pain. Rather, it will deepen, because it opens up the indescribable reality of victims.

To the oppressors, Jesus' blood symbolizes the protest, confrontation, and challenge of the oppressed and of God. It participates in the outcries of victims. Like Abel's blood, Jesus' blood cries out from the ground until its voice is heard. It has the extraordinary strength to open up the cruelty of injustice, violence, vice, and evil—to unlock oppressors' hearts of stone.

How does Jesus' blood open up the hearts of the oppressors that otherwise are closed? Jesus' blood as a symbol—organic and living—represents the collective voice of numerous victims crying out for justice and truth. With the chorus of protest, the symbol pierces deaf ears and moves the mountains of unmoving hearts and indifference. It is due to the strength of the presence of the Holy Spirit working through the symbol. The symbol of Jesus' blood involves the transforming work of the Holy Spirit. In actuality, the visible collective symbol of Jesus' blood and the invisible transformative work of the Holy Spirit cooperate for the liberation of victims and the salvation of the oppressors.

PART 2

The Triune Atonement

The atonement theories described in part 1 endeavor to articulate how Jesus' blood brings about salvation for sinners, but most of them basically leave untouched the issue of the liberation of victims and their healing. The exception is the nonviolent narrative atonement theory.[1] Jesus' death is for both the sinned-against and sinners. The death of Martin Luther King Jr. illustrates Jesus' death. King raised public consciousness of racial justice, led the civil rights movement in the United States, and was killed by the injustice of racism. His civil rights movement has changed civil laws, discriminatory social practices, political agendas, structural systems of racism, and people's consciousness on racial issues. His nonviolent resistance has helped the restructuring of the minds of both African Americans and European Americans. A number of European Americans have publicly acknowledged how much King's movement has liberated them from their prejudices. In this sense, he died for African Americans, European Americans, and other ethnic people.[2] His death transformed the racial conscience of the nation and beyond.

Let me further illustrate Jesus' atonement with a story. There were two brothers living with their old mother. One day a severe argument broke out because of an inheritance dispute. Unable to control his anger and greed, the older son became violent and, wielding a big stick, intended to hit his brother. The mother tried to stop her older son but put herself in the way and was struck to the floor by a blow from the stick. As she lay bleeding and dying, the older son rushed to his mother and held her in his arms, crying in confusion and sorrow. In dying, she forgave the son and commanded him to repent of his greed and violence and to seek his younger brother's forgiveness. To the younger brother she pleaded for him to forgive his older brother. Then she died.

Jesus may be compared to this mother who loves both of her sons. Jesus cares for both victims and perpetrators. Jesus' life, death, and resurrection bring forth salvation and liberation to sinners and victims. God cares about God's children whether they are the sinned-against or the sinners.

Jesus came to transform the world. He cares for both the sinned-against and the sinner. Jesus' atonement has two indivisible dimensions that are intertwined with each other. We will now examine Jesus' death from the perspective of the victims of sin first, and then from the perspective of sinners or oppressors. Since this aspect of victims has been overlooked by traditional theories of the atonement, we will pay more attention to this perspective. At the end of the book, we will treat the groaning of animals and of nature and the meaning of Jesus' work for them.

Jesus' Atonement for Victims
and the Oppressed

When we talk about Jesus' blood, we usually think of it as
being shed for sinners. As a matter of fact, the Gospels tell us
that Jesus primarily lived among the marginalized, served
them, and experienced their deep agony. He suffered with
them and opposed the exploitation and oppression of the religious and political authorities and died for the causes of justice
and divine rule for the sake of the downtrodden. Jesus' life and
death can be explained with the Korean term *han*.

HAN AND JESUS' CROSS

What is *han*? In Korean, *han* is a deep, unhealed wound of a
victim that festers in her or him. It can be a social, economic,
political, physical, mental, or spiritual wound generated by
political oppression, economic exploitation, social alienation,
cultural contempt, injustice, poverty, or war. It may be a deep
ache, an intense bitterness, or the sense of helplessness, hopelessness, or resignation at the individual and collective levels.

Han can be seen in the survivors of the Nazi holocaust,
the Palestinians in the occupied lands, the hungry, the racially
discriminated-against, unemployed workers, battered wives,
the molested, the abused, the exploited, the despised, or the
dehumanized.

Han is a frustrated hope. Hope is the foundation of our
existence: *ex* (out) and *sistere* (cause to stand). Human beings
exist because we stand out. This means that we exist in hope.
Only when we look out, look forward, and look up, we exist.
When hope is frustrated, it turns into *han*, producing sadness,

resignation, resentment, and helplessness. Suffering persons
need to go through grief, but when victims are boxed in and
suffer with no exit by means of grief, *han* develops.[3]

Arirang is a Koran folk song that is about three hundred
years old. It is the song of *han*.

> Refrain: Arirang, Arirang Arai Yo! Crossing the hill of
>   Arirang.
>
> Verse 1:   If you forsake me, you will have sore feet
>   before reaching one mile.
>
> Verse 2:   In the blue sky are many stars and in my
>   heart, many sorrows.
>
> Verse 3:   Arirang is the mountain of sorrow; the path to
>   Arirang has no returning.[4]

Here is a hidden story behind the song:

> Near Seoul is a hill called the Hill of Arirang. During the
> oppressive Li dynasty there was a giant solitary pine at the
> top of this hill, and this was the official place of execution for
> several hundred years. Tens of thousands of prisoners were
> hanged on a gnarled branch of that ancient tree, their bodies
> suspended over a cliff at the side. Some were bandits. Some
> were common criminals, Some were dissidents and scholars.
> Some were political and family enemies of the emperor.
> Many were poor farmers who had raised their fists against
> oppression. Many were rebel youths who had struggled
> against tyranny and injustice. The story is that one of those
> young men composed a song during his imprisonment, and
> as he trudged slowly up the Hill of Arirang, he sang this
> song. The people learned it, and after that whenever a man
> was condemned to die he sang this in fare well to his joys or
> sorrows. . . . It is a song of death and not of life. But death is
> not defeat. Out of many deaths victory may be born.[5]

C. S. Song says, "If Jesus had known the song of Arirang, he
would have sung it as he trudged along the road to Calvary."[6]
Arirang is the song of Golgotha and the song of *han*ful victims.

The story of Cain and Abel (Gen. 4:1–16) is the story of *han*. The two brothers gave offerings to God. Cain's offering was rejected, but Abel's was accepted. Out of his deep jealousy and frustration, Cain struck down his own brother. Then God asked Cain, "Where is your brother Abel?" He replied, "I do not know; am I my brother's keeper?" (v. 9). And God said, "What have you done? Listen; your brother's blood is crying out to me from the ground!" (v. 10). The blood that cried out from the ground is the voice of *han*.

Han has three levels: individual, collective, and structural. At its individual level, it is a response to individualistic oppression, which is often connected to collective and structural oppression. At its collective level, *han* is the collective consciousness and unconsciousness of victims, such as the ethos of a cultural inferiority complex, racial lamentation, racial resentment, the sense of physical inadequacy, and national shame. At its structural level, it is a chronic sense of helplessness and resignation before powerful monopolistic capitalism, pervasive racism, tenacious sexism, and oppressive classism.

Sin or injustice causes *han*, and *han* produces sin or injustice.[7] The sin of the oppressors may cause a chain reaction via the *han* of the oppressed. Sometimes *han* causes *han*. Furthermore, unattended or unhealed *han* gives rise to evil. This evil can regenerate *han* and sin. Also, sin and *han* collaborate to engender evil. They overlap in many tragic areas of life.

For victims of injustice, Jesus came to liberate and heal them from their *han*. Unto death, Jesus challenged social wrongs for the sake of the sinned-against, announcing the coming of God's reign. He laid down his life after standing up for their liberation from religious injustice, economic exploitation, political oppression, and social contempt. As a result of his work for the downtrodden, he was marked, arrested, and executed. On the cross, he cried out with a loud voice, "Eloi, Eloi, lema sabachthani [My God, my God, why have you forsaken me]?" (Mark 15:34). He experienced God's abandonment as the victims of sin and violence did. His outcry over God's forsaking him in time of trouble is the voice of the *han* of victims. The living Jesus and the Paraclete respond to the outcry of the *han* of victims.

JESUS' CROSS AS HIS SOLIDARITY WITH VICTIMS

During his life, Jesus sided with the downtrodden. Jesus tried to empower victims to free themselves from violence, injustice, exploitation, and oppression by identifying with them. However, he was ridiculed, rejected, persecuted, prosecuted, and executed in shame and disgrace. His suffering on the cross exposed the agony and pain of wronged victims and the ugliness, violence, unfairness, and cruelty of wrongdoers.

Solidarity signifies sharing a common goal, communal identity, commiseration, and liberative work.[8] First, solidarity starts when people share a common goal of life together. Jesus' mission statement clearly shows the goal of his ministry: "'The Spirit of the Lord is upon me, because he has anointed me to bring good news to the poor. He has sent me to proclaim release to the captives and recovery of sight to the blind, to let the oppressed go free, to proclaim the year of the Lord's favor.' . . . Then he began to say to them, 'Today this scripture has been fulfilled in your hearing'" (Luke 4:18–21). His mission focuses on the deliverance of the poor, the captives, the blind, and the oppressed. The downtrodden gathered around him and followed him. He implemented this statement into his daily practice throughout his life. Even his death and resurrection must be interpreted in view of his mission statement. He was primarily concerned about the liberation of the oppressed through his life.

Second, Jesus identified with the downtrodden. The parable of the Last Judgment (Matt. 25:31–46) clearly demonstrates how much Jesus identified himself with the poor, oppressed, imprisoned, hungry, and thirsty. In fact, Jesus himself was one of the downtrodden.

Regarding his social status, Jesus was a carpenter or a construction worker, a *tektōn* (Mark 6:3). In the contemporary

West, carpenters are well-paid members of the middle class. At the time of Jesus, *tektōn* belonged to a lower class. The upper classes included the ruler and the governors, who owned at least half of the land (1 percent of the population); the priests, who had possession of 15 percent of the land; the retainers, who ranged from military generals to expert bureaucrats; and the merchants, who probably evolved from the lower classes and possessed considerable wealth and some political power. The lower classes comprised the peasants, who supported the upper classes with two-thirds of their annual crop and barely supported their own families, animals, and social obligations (the vast majority of the population); the artisans, who were recruited and replenished from the dispossessed members of the peasants (5 percent of the population); and the degraded and expendable classes, who ranged from beggars and outlaws to hustlers, day laborers, and slaves (10 percent).[9] As a manual worker (*tektōn*), Jesus belonged to the artisan class. Jesus was one of the marginalized at that time.[10]

Third, Jesus commiserated with the marginalized by carrying their *han*. His death is vicarious in the sense that he lived, died, and rose to liberate them from oppression and injustice: "This was to fulfill what had been spoken through the prophet Isaiah, 'He took our infirmities and bore our diseases'" (Matt. 8:17). It is interesting to see what the Matthean author says: what he has borne is not our sin or iniquity but our infirmities and diseases—*han*. Jesus shed his blood to bear our *han*.

As one of the downtrodden, Jesus went through their agony, advocated for their rights, and healed their *han*, standing with them in their suffering. Jesus Christ becomes their truest friend, who understands their pain and agony and touches their sorrow. He stands firm with them in this *han*-ridden life.

Throughout his life, Jesus bore the frailties and weaknesses of the downtrodden. We ought not to separate his life from their affliction and misery. If we isolate his life from the lives of the downtrodden, his crucifixion cannot be fully understood or properly interpreted. His life, death, and resurrection are interwoven with the healing and liberating of people.

Fourth, Jesus liberated people from the powers and principalities of disease, social illness, and religious manipulation
through performing miracles that released people from their
bondage of suffering. Jesus' miracles involved the expulsion of
demons. The Letter to the Ephesians describes the evil powers
well: "For our struggle is not against enemies of blood and
flesh, but against the rulers, against the authorities, against the
cosmic powers of this present darkness, against the spiritual
forces of evil in the heavenly places" (6:12). Jesus came to
release the ill-treated from destitution, injustice, fear, exploitation, religious legalism, and evil powers. Healing and deliverance are inseparable. By healing the sick and the hurt, he
delivered them from bondage. His healing and deliverance
served the purpose of his proclamation for the advancement of
God's reign on earth. Jesus' ministry put the accent on the healing of the wounded and the deliverance of the downtrodden by
resolving their *han*.

Healing, however, is different from curing. Curing means
"getting well" from diseases. Healing is more inclusive: it has
physical, mental, and spiritual dimensions. It is a deliverance
from the bondage of illness, from fragmentary life, from mean-
inglessness, or from hopelessness. It can take place in the midst
of suffering and struggling without cure. People who are cured
from their illness may not be healed. Nine out of the ten lepers
were cured but not healed (Luke 17:11–19). The Samaritan
leper was genuinely healed: "Get up and go on your way; your
faith has made you well" (v. 19).[11]

Jesus healed victims by restoring their human dignity and
divine rights. His life proved that he withstood Pharisees'
attacks on so-called sinners. These "sinners" were shepherds,
tanners, the sick, and the poor. In fact, they were the sinned-
against. They were *'am ha'areṣ*, the people of the land, and Jesus
was one of them. He encouraged the downtrodden to free
themselves from the chains of oppression, exploitation, and
domination and helped them transcend their hatred, bitterness, and unforgiving hearts toward their oppressors. Jesus confronted the injustice of the powerful in Jerusalem and tried to

set the oppressed free from the systems of religious and socio-economic exploitation: "Woe to you, scribes and Pharisees, hypocrites! For you tithe mint, dill, and cumin, and have neglected the weightier matters of the law: justice and mercy and faith" (Matt. 23:23). He did not put up with the economic abuses of religious leaders and passionately expressed his disapproval of them. It was very difficult for religious leaders to allow Jesus to go on with his new movement. Thus, they determined to remove him at their earliest chance. In this sense, Jesus truly laid down his life to deliver the abused from injustice and evil. He embodied what he had preached: "No one has greater love than this, to lay down one's life for one's friends" (John 15:13). His liberation work emerged from his great love for his downtrodden friends. Even after his death, his new movement grew more strongly, empowering the downtrodden to be God's daughters and sons.

In conclusion, Jesus' life and death point to God's solidarity with the *han*-ridden. They provide the foundation of his oneness with them to overcome *han*—the absurdity, falsehood, violence, and death of everyday life—with courage, justice, truth, benevolence, and dignity.

Jesus' outcry "My God, my God, why have you forsaken me?" echoes every victim's outcry. When a hungry child cries in starvation, a child is sexually or physically abused or molested, a child is despised and discriminated against because of the color of his or her skin, a woman is raped, a homosexual person is murdered, a poor person shivers in the cold, a prisoner in a dungeon is tortured, a person is injured or killed in a war, or an AIDS victim dies, Jesus' shrill outcry "My God, my God, why have you forsaken me?" reverberates across the valley of the shadow of death.

JESUS' CROSS AS THE SYMBOL OF CHALLENGE

To the victims of wrong, Jesus' life and death show them how to challenge injustice, wrong, and evil. Jesus challenged the injustices of his society with care. If he did not care about his society, he could have been silent about the injustices of Israel, or he could have escaped into the Jordan desert. Since he was dearly concerned about people, he confronted evil unto death.

Jesus' death is the complete expression of his challenge to religious oppression, social injustice, economic exploitation, violence, and killing. Matthew 23 shows how visceral Jesus was toward the Pharisees' and scribes' religious legalism and economic exploitation. Jesus emphatically denounced the fact that they tithed mint, dill, and cumin but neglected the weightier matters of the law: justice and mercy and faith (23:23). He warned the scribes not to devour widows' houses (Mark 12:40). Because of his ministry of social justice and confrontation, the religious leaders sought to get rid of him.

His life was a series of challenges to religious legalism, social custom, economic injustice, and political tyranny. His saying no to these reverberates from Galilee to every valley of the shadow of unequal treatment of human beings, domination, violence, and death. Such a voice of resistance continues in Martin Luther's *Nein* to the Roman Catholic hierarchy, Martin Niemöller's *Nein* to the Nazi regime, and Rosa Parks's no to the unjust rule of segregation.

Saying no may require risking one's life. Jesus' death showed the ultimate courage in throwing injustice out from the world. Jesus stuck out his neck to advance the reign of God by saying no to the injustices of the religious and political establishments. In this sense, Jesus' crucifixion stands by our side when we say no to injustice.

There are two kinds of no. One is the cynical no that tears down one's opponent, and is based on hatred. The other is the constructive no that tries to change the wrong of one's opponent, and is based on care. Jesus' confrontation is the symbol of the constructive no of grace. Jesus refused to be silent about the religious terrors, the combination of graft and political power, the corruption of temple practices, social discrimination, and armed resistance or revolution.

Nonviolent Challenge

Jesus' challenge was his language of love to straighten out the oppressors and to change oppressive systems. He taught his followers how to treat enemies by resisting their evil. His teaching of the Sermon on the Mount shows how we can challenge our enemies by standing up to their inhuman assaults with human dignity and care.

Jesus asked his followers not to resist an evildoer (*tō ponērō*), but to return evil with good. Here the term *resist (antistenai)* should be understood as an armed uprising. Jesus unmistakably prohibited the armed resistance that the Zealots carried out but commanded a nonviolent resistance ("returning evil with good"). His teaching on turning the other cheek, giving the cloak, and going the second mile shows us how to resist evil with good:

> You have heard that it was said, "An eye for an eye and a tooth for a tooth." But I say to you, Do not resist an evildoer. But if anyone strikes you on the right cheek, turn the other also; and if anyone wants to sue you and take your coat, give your cloak as well; and if anyone forces you to go one mile, go also the second mile. (Matt. 5:38–41)

Jesus preached this message to the poor Galileans. They were marginalized by the Jewish and Roman authorities. To them, Jesus delivered his essential message of nonviolent resistance of love. Loving our oppressors or persecutors does not mean permitting them to continue undisturbed in their unjust practices. It is the effort to change the unjust into the just.[12] Jesus teaches us how to deal with the evildoers.

First, "turn the other cheek" signifies active protest. "But if anyone strikes you on the right cheek, turn the other also" (Matt. 5:39). Slapping on the right cheek may mean a strike with the back of the hand or with the left hand.[13] Either would have been a sharp insult in Jewish custom, for the left hand was regarded as unclean based on its use for toilet purposes, and the back of the hand was used for insulting someone. A slap by the back of one's hand required a double penalty as satisfaction for it.[14] The Mishnah, the oldest authoritative collection of Jewish oral law, imposes the fine for a slap with the back of the hand: "If a man slapped his fellow, he gives him 200 *zuz*: if with the back of this hand, 400 *zuz*."[15] The slapping of the face suggests an insult rather than an injury. Masters used the backhand slap to humiliate slaves; husbands, wives; parents, children; Romans, Jews. If the superior struck the inferior with the flat side of the right hand on the left cheek, such an act meant to end the intention of humiliation. Thus, turning the left cheek signified the act of demanding for equality and for the end of dehumanization.[16] It was an active form of resistance.

Jesus clearly shows by example the meaning of turning the other cheek. When a policeman strikes Jesus on the face, accusing him for his improper response to the high priest, Jesus answers, "If I have spoken wrongly, testify to the wrong. But if I have spoken rightly, why do you strike me?" (John 18:23). He did not turn the other cheek but protested the injustice. Total surrender to the enemy's unjust actions or demands can hardly be called love.[17]

Second, Jesus teaches the oppressed what to do when someone wants to sue and take their tunics: "If anyone wants to sue you and take your coat, give your cloak as well" (Matt. 5:40). This case alludes to the common Jewish practice of pawning a debtor's garment as a pledge. What is unusual in this case is the fact that the creditor sues the debtor to get the coat or undergarment (*chitōn*). Since Moses' law prohibits a creditor from pawning a debtor's outer garment or cloak (*himation*) overnight because its owner may need to use it as a blanket at night, this creditor goes after the undergarment. Creditors needed to return cloaks by sunset: "If you lend money to my people, to the poor among you, you shall not deal with them as a creditor. . . . If you take your neighbor's cloak in pawn, you shall restore it before the sun goes down; for it may be your neighbor's only clothing to use as cover" (Exod. 22:25–27). Further, Deuteronomy prohibits anyone to pawn a poor person's cloak overnight: "If the person is poor, you shall not sleep in the garment given you as the pledge. You shall give the pledge back by sunset, so that your neighbor may sleep in the cloak and bless you" (Deut. 24:12–13). But this law does not apply to the coat or undergarment. Thus, the evil one goes after the coat in this case.

In response to such a calculated demand, Jesus teaches the defender to give away both the undergarment and the outer garment. This means parading out of court completely naked. Nakedness was taboo in Israel. However, the shame of nakedness in this case would fall not on the person without clothing, but on the one who caused that person to go naked. This act of disrobing would unmask the cruelty of the creditor and the entire system that oppresses the poor debtor. To Walter Wink, the poor say by the action, "You want my robe? Here, take everything! Now you've got all I have except my body. Is that what you'll take next?"[18] Challenge demands an explanation, or the doing of justice; it calls the unjust act into question. It is not a Machiavellian act that schemes to put the offender to public shame. Rather, it is an act of courage that faces injustice and evil with truth.

Third, the act of going the second mile (Matt. 5:41) could be an act of defiance. Roman soldiers had the legal right to impose forced labor on subjected peoples, requiring them to carry their bags up to one mile. To do this, however, the soldiers needed written permits from the prefect. The soldiers abused these rules, stirring up resentment, which in turn led the Roman authorities to punish violators. Wink contends that in this context, Jesus' teaching was neither to aid nor to abet the enemy. Carrying a soldier's package the second mile could be interpreted several ways: "Is this a provocation? Is he insulting the legionnaire's strength? Being kind? Trying to get him disciplined for seeming to violate the rules of impressment? Will this civilian file a complaint? Create trouble?"[19] It could lead to an ironic situation in which a Roman soldier pleads with the laborer to return his baggage.

Wink is convinced that Jesus did not mean his fellow Jews to walk a second mile in order to pile up merit in heaven, or to practice a supererogative piety, or to smother the soldier with kindness. Rather, he was trying to help the oppressed protest and neutralize the unjust practice of the impressed labor.[20]

Wink believes that Jesus counseled neither flight (submission, passivity, withdrawal, and surrender) nor fight (armed revolt, violent rebellion, direct retaliation, and revenge). Instead, Jesus taught a third way: find a creative alternative to violence, assert your own humanity and dignity as a person, meet force with ridicule or humor, break the cycle of humiliation, refuse to accept the inferior position, expose the injustice of the system, shame oppressors into repentance, stand your ground, recognize your own power, force the oppressor to see you in a new light, deprive the oppressor of a situation where a show of force is effective, be willing to undergo the penalty of breaking unjust laws, seek the oppressor's transformation, and so on.[21]

Wink sums up Jesus' third way in the following sentence: "Jesus, in short, abhors both passivity and violence. He articulates, out of the history of his own people's struggles, a way by which evil can be opposed without being mirrored, the oppressor resisted without being emulated, and the enemy neutralized without being destroyed."[22]

Richard Horsley agrees with Wink that Jesus' strategy in Matthew 5:39–42 was socially revolutionary, but disagrees with him on the notion that the focal point of the sayings was not whether the strategy was violent or nonviolent but whether it was focused on the renewal of local communities or not. Horsley contends that in the broad social-historical context, Jesus addressed the issue for the improvement of local communities, not for the amelioration of the relations between oppressed Jews and oppressive Romans or Jews.[23]

For Horsley, the backhanded insult was not limited to the relations between the superior and the inferior, but could address the issues of local quarrels and conflicts. Since slapping on the cheek was a formal and serious insult, not a spontaneous action of violence or "damage to person," the context of this saying is the local village.[24] Also, since Matt. 5:40 refers to the case of the seizure of a garment as a pledge, the saying manifests a local interaction between creditor and debtor: "The creditor asking for the cloak would more likely have been a local than a wealthy absentee official or landowner."[25] As to going the second mile, Horsley has doubts about Wink's sociopolitical context of the occupied troops. He holds that since Galilee was ruled by the client king Antipas, it is unlikely that the Galileans were burdened by the presence of Roman soldiers.

Wink's rebuttal is that we cannot confine the perimeter of the application of Jesus' teaching to local compatriots. Jesus taught people to love their enemies in reference to the Romans as well as their puppets.[26] While Wink stresses that these passages are aimed at the relationships between oppressed Jews and oppressive Jews or Romans, Horsley emphasizes that they focus on the relationships of local people.

I believe that Jesus' teaching could be applied to any relationships between villagers, between the Romans and the occupied, or between creditors and debtors. It is clear, however, that Jesus addressed these sayings to the offended, not offenders. He wished to instruct the violated how to react. Since Jesus' audience largely belonged to a lower class, he had compassion for their situations.

Our motivation to challenge evil forces is not only for our own liberation but also to change our opponents with a resilient caring spirit. Jesus taught us to withstand wrongs in order to lead wrongdoers to their repentance. It is easy for us to receive the slap on the right cheek, say nothing, and avoid our oppressor, all the while regarding him or her with brooding hatred. It is a different matter to confront the oppressor with justice and care. Only the care that humanizes our enemy enables us to deal with him or her again. By turning the other cheek, we demand justice and equality from our oppressor and enter into an ongoing relationship with him or her. Only when we care enough for the oppressor can we challenge him or her to change. This care for the oppressor becomes the essential ingredient in challenge. Without it, confrontation would turn into hatred and retaliation, dehumanizing us and failing to change the oppressor.

Based on God's justice, Jesus' teaching on nonviolent challenge is implemented in the event of his crucifixion. Jesus' crucifixion is the greatest challenge of God to the oppressors. It demands that oppressors stop wielding their abusive power. The cross is the concrete historical emblem of God's suffering because of the sins of oppressors or sinners. The cross does not condemn the oppressors but rebukes the falsehood, manipulation, and dark side of their power. It urges the oppressors to turn away from these and to come back to God's rule.

Let us see concretely how Jesus challenged evil in his life. Jesus' lifetime activities, particularly those of the final week in Jerusalem, can be interpreted in the light of resistance. Jesus was a great threat to the religious and political power of Caiaphas and his group. Caiaphas plotted to kill Jesus by running a sham trial and convicted him of blasphemy. There are several reasons why he wanted to kill Jesus.

Challenge to Economic Exploitation

Jesus challenged the authority of Caiaphas and the high priests over the commerce in the temple court. As Jesus entered Jerusalem, he defied the practices of people in the temple by interrupting their business: "And he entered the temple and began to drive out those who were selling and those who were buying in the temple, and he overturned the tables of the money changers and the seats of those who sold doves" (Mark 11:15). He upset the seats and the tables of the temple businesspeople. The law required unpolluted animals and birds for sacrifice, and people conveniently purchased those animals from nearby authorized places sanctioned by the temple priests. In fact, there were times they purchased a pair of doves outside the temple, it cost fifteen times less than inside.[27] However, because of purity laws, people had to buy both animals and birds in the temple.

Furthermore, diaspora Jews from all across the world upheld the temple by paying their annual taxes; the money changers offered to exchange a number of foreign currencies into the single official coinage. In effect, says John Dominic Crossan, the temple functioned as the U.S. Federal Reserve Bank at that time.[28]

Every man annually paid a temple tax of half a shekel (= two drachmas or six *maahs*), nearly two days' wages for a laborer. A month before Passover, people could pay the tax in their own towns, but pilgrims who came to the Passover feast paid the tax in Jerusalem. They had to pay the temple tax of a half-shekel in "silver didrachmas of Tyre."[29] Since they came from Greece, Rome, Tyre, Syria, and Egypt, they needed money changers. The booths for money changing were controlled by chief priests. The money changers charged one *maah* to change a coin of exact value.[30] If a larger coin was tendered, they charged another *maah*. This was a deliberate system of imposing on the poor who could afford it least.[31]

By driving out the merchants and upsetting the tables of the money changers, Jesus stopped the flow of the bank system.

Moreover, Jesus also threatened a useful source of income for the temple priests. The temple operation yielded enormous revenues for simple rituals for purification and the forgiveness of sins. Before participating in worship, worshipers purified themselves by using ritual baths. Archaeologists have excavated 150 ritual baths around the temple.[32]

Almost all Jewish people traveling to Jerusalem for Passover were ritually polluted. To satisfy their religious requirements, they needed to use the ritual baths. The priests regulated the processes of ritual purification and the fees of ritual baths as a means of harvesting money.

Jesus directly confronted the authorities by treating these practices as hogwash. To him, it was unnecessary for people to go through painstaking purity rituals to inherit eternal life. God requires their repenting hearts and love, not observing the external rituals of the temple by paying for ritual baths and offering sacrificial animals. Jesus never offered sacrifices for himself or for his disciples. Accusing the merchants of turning the temple into a robbers' den, he drove them out of it. His actions and words were saying that people were exploited by the temple systems. This elicited a response that could have exploded into a revolt at any time. Caiaphas and his associates had to do something before it got out of hand. They decided to remove Jesus.

In addition, we find Jesus impeding the passageway of the temple court to any businesspeople in Mark 11:16: "He would not allow anyone to carry anything through the temple." Although Jesus is depicted as acting alone, this passage implies the collaboration of his disciples in blocking the temple gates. This meant the paralysis of all commerce in the temple court. Although alarmed by Jesus' use of physical force, Caiaphas and the Sanhedrin members did not intervene in his blockade.

Caiaphas restrained himself in counteracting Jesus' audacious acts during the daytime because people regarded him as a prophet. Jesus could not stand such injustice and drove out the merchants from the temple.

Challenge to Religious Authorities

Jesus undermined the authority and stability of the religious leaders by threatening the symbolic destruction of the temple. The temple was the center of the Sadducees' activities. It symbolized the religious well-being of the Israelites.

For John Dominic Crossan, Mark's purpose in including the temple cleansing account is to show us that Jesus was symbolically destroying the temple. This was presaged in the destruction of the fig tree during the morning of the temple purification: "When he came to it, he found nothing but leaves, for it was not the season for figs. He said to it, 'May no one ever eat fruit from you again.' And his disciples heard it" (Mark 11:13-14). After this incident he entered the temple and symbolically demolished it by attacking its economic, sacrificial, and cultic activities. The next morning, the disciples saw the fig tree withered away to its roots (Mark 11:20–21). To Crossan, Jesus did not clean or purify the temple but symbolically destroyed it. Furthermore, God ratified Jesus' action by deserting the temple's inner sanctuary through a symbolic act of abandoning it: "And the curtain of the temple was torn in two, from top to bottom" (Mark 15:38).[33]

Jesus, however, focused on the function of the temple as a house of prayer, although his anti-temple attitude was clearly shown. He attacked the unjust temple trades against Gentile worshipers, stressing the proper role of the temple: "Is it not written, 'My house shall be called a house of prayer for all the nations'? But you have made it a den of robbers" (Mark 11:17).

Mark alone mentions the temple as a house of prayer for "all the nations." The temple was divided into several courts: first the Court of the Gentiles, then the Court of the Women, then the Court of the Israelites, and then the Court of the Priests. All the hustle and bustle of business transactions took place in the Court of the Gentiles. The Gentiles who came for meditation or prayer could not do so because of all the loud selling and buying. They were not allowed to go beyond their court. Trespassing beyond their court meant death. The temple authorities and the traders turned the Court of the Gentiles into an open marketplace where no Gentile could worship God. Jesus confronted this Jewish exclusivism toward the Gentiles—the uncaring attitudes and haughtiness—by claiming the temple as the house of prayer for all the nations.[34]

It is noteworthy that Jesus uses the term "house" to refer to the temple several times (two times in Mark and two times in John). He clearly saw the main role of the temple as the house of true worship for all peoples, not as the place of cultic rituals for the Israelites alone. Matthew reports Jesus' anticultic remarks twice in different situations. When he was accused of being a friend of sinners, when he ate with tax collectors, he said, "Go and learn what this means, 'I desire mercy, not sacrifice.' For I have come to call not the righteous but sinners" (Matt. 9:13). When he and his disciples were accused of breaking the sabbatical law, Jesus said, "But if you had known what this means, 'I desire mercy and not sacrifice,' you would not have condemned the guiltless" (Matt. 12:7).

These two incidents disclose Jesus' negative attitude toward sacrificial rituals. His emphasis on anticultic teaching and the anti-temple system seriously threatened the religious authorities.

His healing on the Sabbath was an act of challenge to the Jewish religious authorities. In the environment where the violation of the Sabbath could be punished with death ("Whoever does any work on it shall be put to death," Exod. 35:2), Jesus' action was a deadly serious challenge to the Jewish religious authorities.

On the Sabbath, healing was forbidden. Even a fracture or cuts could not be healed, but could be only put off from getting worse. Jesus knew well the prohibition of healing on the Sabbath. When he asked the people in a synagogue whether it is lawful to do good on the Sabbath day, no one answered (Mark 3:1–6). He looked around on them with anger and grieved at the obtuseness of their hearts, then he ordered the man with the withered hand to stretch out his hand, and Jesus healed it. This was a clear action of challenging the wrong interpretation of the Sabbath that the religious authorities imposed upon people. There were people who came from the Sanhedrin to observe him in the synagogue, and Jesus healed the man's hand before them. The Pharisees immediately went out and conspired with the Herodians against him in order to destroy him (3:6). His religious confrontation was dangerous enough even for the Herodians to partake in the plot to kill him, because religious instability meant political insecurity.

Challenge to Political Power

Jesus also threatened the political status quo. At Passover, a great number of Jews gathered in Jerusalem. It was a volatile time.[35] Jesus made a strap and drove all of the merchants out of the temple, with the sheep and the oxen, and he poured out the coins of the money changers and overturned their tables (John 2:15). He blocked the temple gates and would not permit anyone to carry merchandise through the temple (Mark 11:16). The populace revered the temple so deeply that they did not mind laying down their lives to keep it pure and honored. At the time of Jesus' birth and after his death, the people tried to defend the purity of the temple up to the point of sacrificing their own lives.[36]

While standing before the crowd of the Passover festival, Jesus accused the religious leaders of letting the temple be infected by commercial corruptions and extortions. It was more a meeting place of thieves than a place of prayer. When the chief priests and the scribes heard this, they feared an eruption of public outrage and rioting because Jesus instigated the crowd to react to the defilement of the temple.

If there were any riots during the Passover festival, Roman legions would be called upon to suppress them. It might have cost the political life of Caiaphas. He was the supreme political leader in Jerusalem. The Sanhedrin was his power hub. Consisting of seventy-one members, mostly chief priests, the Sanhedrin was the supreme council of Jews and ruled over civil and religious law.

Caiaphas, the high priest who survived eighteen years in the post, led the Sanhedrin members. They perceived threats to their security by the actions of Jesus and attempted to avoid trouble with the Romans. Caiaphas could not afford to let this country preacher threaten his political life. At Passover, the biggest Jewish festival, Caiaphas wanted to avoid any chance of losing face.

Jesus confronted the corrupt business practices of the Jewish leaders in the temple with passion, and he compelled them to make reforms. Caiaphas convened a meeting of the chief priests. According to Matthew's Gospel, Caiaphas conspired with them to put Jesus to death.

The priests, however, were not at all sure about the timing. They wanted to avoid the Passover festival. If Jesus were killed, there might be riots. However, when Judas betrayed Jesus, Caiaphas jumped at the opportunity to implement the conspiracy immediately. He had the temple guards arrest Jesus that very night and put him on trial before the high court.

Here Caiaphas himself began to violate Jewish laws. He mocked the trial by bending several Jewish laws. He conducted the trial in his house at night (according to Mark and Matthew) during the Passover, playing the double role of prosecutor and judge. (Luke reports that the trial happened in the morning. This creates a problem of timing for three trials in Friday morning: the trials before Caiaphas, Herod, and Pilate.) Caiaphas should have tried Jesus in the council chamber during the day after Passover, taking the role of the supreme judge.

The trial went awry for Caiaphas. He tried to prove Jesus' threat to destroy the temple, which would have been a crime of treason and an offense to God. As Caiaphas failed to indict Jesus on those grounds, he intervened and asked Jesus directly: "Are you the Messiah, the Son of the Blessed One?" (Mark 14:61). Jesus' answer, "I am," was sufficient for Caiaphas to declare him guilty of blasphemy; the court seconded him. To them Jesus deserved death. Since the Romans alone could execute a criminal, this involved Pilate, the procurator.

Pilate desperately needed the cooperation of the Jewish leaders to maintain peace in the city, for his political life was contingent upon his undisturbed and trouble-free rule of the province.

At Passover, Pilate had to control a Jerusalem that swelled into large crowds of people with a small number of soldiers. Caiaphas and the Sanhedrin sought the execution of Jesus, and the angry masses demanded Jesus' blood. After interrogating Jesus, Pilate learned that Jesus was not a violent revolutionary or a zealot, although he might be politically dangerous. Releasing Jesus, however, could cause a riot and the loss of Pilate's control over Jerusalem. Caiaphas and the Sanhedrin accused Jesus of political agitation: "We found this man perverting our nation, and forbidding us to pay tribute to the emperor, and saying that he himself is the Messiah, a king" (Luke 23:2).

Pilate, calculating and shrewd, made up his mind and condemned Jesus as a political insurgent for the preservation of Roman rule and his own career. Jesus was sentenced to death as a Jewish political messiah.

Caiaphas, the Sanhedrin, and Pilate used Jesus as a political scapegoat to keep the political stability of the region. They feared that Jesus might stir up a revolt and bring forth a real threat to their political lives and survival. Jesus disregarded their attempt to survive by holding on to power through relying upon a stronger power—the Roman Empire.

Jesus defied the power that people worshiped. He challenged Pilate to think of the source of power as something beyond the empire. There is authentic power in life. That is truth. For Jesus, truth was the true power he wanted people to seek after, not political and military power:

> Jesus answered, "My kingdom is not from this world. If my kingdom were from this world, my followers would be fighting to keep me from being handed over to the Jews. But as it is, my kingdom is not from here." Pilate asked him, "So you are a king?" Jesus answered, "You say that I am a king. For this I was born, and for this I came into the world, to testify to the truth. Everyone who belongs to the truth listens to my voice." Pilate asked him, "What is truth?" (John 18:36–38)

Jesus came to witness to the truth, and he did so both to the people and to Pilate. His death is a direct challenge to people's misplaced worship of political power. Jesus was killed because he declined to compromise with political power and defied it with the power of truth. He was born to teach and to die for truth, and he did both.

Jesus strongly resisted the political power of Herod Antipas, king of Galilee. Jesus warned his disciples against the leaven of the Pharisees and of Herod Antipas (Mark 8:15). After Herod Antipas ordered John beheaded, he was going to kill Jesus also. When some Pharisees came and warned him that Herod had been seeking to kill him, Jesus responded to them, "Go and tell

that fox for me, 'Listen, I am casting out demons and performing cures today and tomorrow, and on the third day I finish my
work" (Luke 13:32). The fox symbolized three things to the
Jews. First, it was the slyest of animals. Second, it was the most
destructive of animals. Third, it was a worthless and insignificant human being.[37] It was a courageous act to call the ruling
king a fox, but Jesus was unafraid of challenging political
authorities. When he met Herod Antipas during his trial, he
defied Herod's command to answer a series of questions and to
perform miracles (Luke 23:9). Silence and noncooperation
were his way of resisting injustice and oppression.

Jesus resisted the unjust system of power worship, political
maneuvering, conspiracy, and compromise. He knew that he
would be killed if he should confront this system. The priests
and scribes exploited the people with all kinds of shrewd political and religious traps. In spite of being aware that he would be
killed if he challenged their systems, he went on with his work
of confrontation.

His life and death teach us how to love our enemies through
nonviolent confrontation, challenge, or resistance. During his last
week, Jesus particularly demonstrated how to resist injustice,
exploitation, and oppression with dignity, courage, and truth.
Like Jesus, victims must challenge injustice and evil without losing the fundamental principle of love. Confrontation or challenge
is not a choice but rather part of discipleship for Jesus' followers
in the face of injustice. Resisting evil with good is the daily cross
we have to take up in order to follow Jesus. The goal is not to
retaliate or destroy the offender, but to help him or her be penitent. Jesus' blood signifies such a challenge of justice and care.

THE LIBERATIVE AND HEALING WORK
OF THE TWINS: JESUS AND THE PARACLETE

Jesus' liberation work is not limited to his death, but is also
extended to his resurrection. His resurrection accelerated the
momentum of his work of salvation, and liberation and healing

started with his public ministry and became full-fledged with his death. The activities of the Paraclete among us since his departure have made his resurrection real and visible.

The Paraclete as the Wounded and Resurrected Holy Spirit

The Holy Spirit had been active before the arrival of the Paraclete. Why did Jesus promise to send the Paraclete? Is the Paraclete different from the Holy Spirit? Are the Paraclete and the Holy Spirit the same? If they are the same, why was it necessary for God to send the Paraclete?

If the Spirit of Jesus is the Holy Spirit, did the Holy Spirit exist before Jesus? Yes, Jesus was *from* the Holy Spirit: "For the child conceived in her is from the Holy Spirit" (Matt. 1:20). Then how could Jesus' Spirit be the Holy Spirit? The Holy Spirit filled Jesus during his earthly life, and the same Holy Spirit embraced Jesus' Spirit after his resurrection.

The Holy Spirit and the Paraclete are the same, but the Paraclete can also be distinguished from the Holy Spirit.

After the crucifixion and the resurrection of Jesus, the Holy Spirit was called the Paraclete in the Johannine writings. It is certain that the Holy Spirit who had been with Jesus before the crucifixion went through the excruciating pain of the trial, the torture, and the crucifixion with Jesus. The Holy Spirit grieved with Jesus and groaned in him, crying out, "My God, my God, why have you forsaken me?" With Jesus, the Holy Spirit sighed and was deeply wounded. The intensity of Jesus' unfair execution developed *han* in the Holy Spirit. The Holy Spirit that underwent suffering with the crucified Jesus is called the Paraclete.

On the third day, Jesus was resurrected. The Paraclete underwent the resurrection with Jesus in exuberant joy. It was a new day and a new beginning in creation.

Subsequently, the Holy Spirit that participated in Jesus' daily life, crucifixion, and resurrection was called the Paraclete after Jesus' departure (John 16:7, 8, 13). Thus, this Paraclete is the wounded and resurrected Holy Spirit that knows the depth of human suffering and grief and the exhilarating joy of the resurrection.[38]

The Paraclete is also more personal than the Holy Spirit in a number of the New Testament passages. While the Holy Spirit, like the Spirit of God in the Hebrew Bible, is energy or a force, the Paraclete is a person.[39]

The Paraclete and the Triune Atonement

The Paraclete has played a key role in the formation of the doctrine of the Trinity and the atonement work of Jesus Christ. The post-Nicene churches believed the Paraclete proceeds from God alone (the Eastern church) and from both God and the Son (the Western church), formulating their understandings of the Trinity. One thing was explicit: the three persons of the Trinity cooperated in their works of atonement. God worked for the fulfillment of the purpose of the creation from the beginning (*creation continua*). Jesus came for the embodiment of the salvation and liberation of the whole creation. The Paraclete continued Jesus' salvific and liberative work. Their works for atonement are triune.

The Holy Spirit is the Spirit of God. It is also the Spirit of Jesus. The Paraclete is the Holy Spirit. The Paraclete has carried out the redemptive and restorative work of Jesus for the past two thousand years. Several decades before the Johannine author used the term *Paraclete,* Paul called the Holy Spirit "the Spirit of God" and "the Spirit of Christ" (Rom. 8:9), "the Spirit of the Son" (Gal. 4:6), or "the Spirit of Jesus" (2 Cor. 3:17; Gal. 4:6; Phil. 1:19). Luke reports that "the Spirit of Jesus" prevented Paul and his associates from going to Bithynia (Acts 16:7). Paul's terms are equivalent to the Johannine author's *Paraclete.*

We read in John: "And I will ask the Father, and he will give you another Advocate, to be with you forever. This is the Spirit of truth, whom the world cannot receive, because it neither sees him nor knows him. You know him, because he abides with you, and he will be in you" (John 14:16–17). "Another Advocate" clearly implies that Jesus has been a Paraclete, since this second Paraclete is coming as Jesus departs.[40] This Paraclete is another Paraclete besides Jesus because she or he takes over the work of Jesus. This Paraclete is different from Jesus because it is neither corporeal nor visible but will indwell in Jesus' followers. The dream of the "Immanuel" of Isaiah (7:14) becomes permanently realized, as this Paraclete will be with us forever.[41]

Another important image of the triune God is found in John 14:23: "Jesus answered and said unto him, If a man love me, he will keep my words: and my Father will love him, and we will come unto him, and make our abode with him" (KJV).

This passage pictures God and Jesus dwelling in those who love them. The doctrine of the mutual indwelling or mutual interpenetration (*perichoresis*) of the Trinity is derived from this passage. *Perichoresis* describes the inseparable relationship between God and Jesus Christ as they dwell in us. St. Hilary of Poitiers (c. 315–c. 368 CE), a disciple of Origen's, was the first to fully and clearly develop this idea of mutual indwelling.[42] In his book *De Trinitate,* Hilary interprets the meaning of John 14:23 through the mutual dwelling:

> For by this He testified that while the Spirit of Christ abides in us the Spirit of God abides in us, and that the Spirit of Him that was raised from the dead differs not from the Spirit of Him that raised Him from the dead. For they come and dwell in us: and I ask whether they will come as alleges associated together and make Their abode, or in unity of nature? . . . This is no joint indwelling, it is one indwelling: yet an indwelling under the mysterious semblance of a joint indwelling, for it is not the case that two Spirits indwell, nor is one that indwells different from the other. For there is in us the Spirit of God and there is also in us the Spirit of Christ, and when the Spirit of Christ is in us there is also in us the Spirit of God. . . . Christ, therefore, is God, one Spirit with God.[43]

Hilary faced the profound mystery of the Trinity with the courage to explain it with paradox and the antithesis of opposite infinities. This relationship between God the Creator and Jesus Christ the Son is one of eternal mutual indwelling, characterized by their oneness of nature and by the infinity of both.

Another important passage concerning the Paraclete is John 15:26: "But when the Comforter is come, whom I will send unto you from the Father, even the Spirit of truth, which proceedeth from the Father, he shall testify of me" (KJV). This passage is the reason why the Western church insisted the procession of the Holy Spirit is from both God the Creator and Jesus Christ. Tertullian (c. 160–c. 225 CE) is the theologian who developed the true formula for the Trinity. In spite of his coinage of the Trinitarian definitive formula, "Three persons, one substance," Tertullian had a clear proclivity to subordinationism.[44] It is extraordinary, however, that Tertullian understood the divinity of the Holy Spirit in a precise manner. In his work *Against Praxeas*, he explicates the nature of the Paraclete. The Paraclete is God, one and the same substance with God and Jesus Christ, proceeding from God through Jesus Christ: "And thus the Spirit is God, and the Word is God, because proceeding from God, but yet is not actually the very same as He from whom He proceeds."[45] To Tertullian, the Paraclete is pivotal to his realization of the idea of the Trinity: "Thus the connection of the Father in the Son, and of the Son in the *Paraclete*, produces three coherent Persons, *who are yet distinct* One from Another. These Three are one *essence*, not one *Person*, as it is said, 'I and my Father are One,' in respect of unity of substance not singularity of number."[46] With such a connection in the Paraclete, Tertullian could build up the idea of the Trinity.

Since the Paraclete is heavily involved in the atonement of humanity and the whole creation, God and Jesus Christ have fully participated in the work of the Paraclete. Jesus said, "My Father is still working, and I also am working" (John 5:17). It is true that since the Paraclete works, God and Jesus Christ work with the Paraclete. In this sense, the atonement is the work of the Trinity. Jesus initiated the atonement movement, and the

Paraclete has carried on after Jesus' departure. God the Creator and Jesus Christ the Redeemer have been fully involved in the atoning work of the Paraclete. This is the reason why we can call this cooperation of interpenetration the "triune atonement."

The Paraclete as Another Jesus

Before his death, Jesus promised that he would ask God to send us another Advocate—the Paraclete: "And I will ask the Father, and he will give you another Advocate, to be with you forever" (John 14:16). As we have seen, Jesus indicated that he himself was the first Paraclete by saying "another." As Jesus is to be in and to remain with the disciples, so does the Paraclete remain in and with them. Whereas unjust people rejected Jesus, so does the world refuse to accept the Paraclete. As Jesus instructed the disciples, so does the Paraclete.

This Paraclete is Jesus' successor as teacher after Jesus' departure (John 14:26).[47] The living presence of Jesus has been experienced in Christian communities through the arrival of the Paraclete. Jesus promised, "I will not leave you orphaned; I am coming to you" (John 14:18).

The Paraclete finally came at Pentecost and has been abiding with us since then. This Paraclete has done the restorative work of Jesus as if he were here on earth. According to Raymond Brown, the Paraclete bridged the gap between the church and Jesus of Nazareth caused by the death of the apostolic eyewitnesses. Furthermore, the arrival of the Paraclete explained the delay of the Parousia, the second coming of Jesus. Due to the arrival of the Paraclete, it was not so disappointing that Jesus had not yet returned by 70 CE, the year of the destruction of Jerusalem. In fact, the arrival of the Paraclete was the valid way of Jesus' returning.[48]

Jesus said that it would be good for him to go away so that the Paraclete might come: "Nevertheless I tell you the truth: it is to your advantage that I go away, for if I do not go away, the Advocate will not come to you; but if I go, I will send him to you" (John 16:7). By sending the Paraclete, Jesus was able to do much more than he could during his lifetime: "Very truly, I tell you, the one who believes in me will also do the works that I do and, in fact, will do greater works than these, because I am going to the Father" (John 14:12). The Paraclete transcends time and space, guiding people to truth and light, healing the hearts of the injured, and teaching people about Jesus' instructions.

The Roles of the Paraclete

The term *Paraclete* etymologically means "called to one's side." As a translation, some scholars use "Comforter," "Helper," "Intercessor," or "Advocate," but it is difficult to translate into a single word. The word *comfort* comes from the Latin *fortis,* "brave," or "strong," and a comforter was the one who made dispirited people brave or strong. The comforter in this sense is different from our common usage, which usually refers to the one who sympathizes with people in sorrow. The Latin *advocatus* pleaded another's case for him or her in a Roman court.

The Greeks employed the word in diverse situations. In a Greek court, the accused had to defend himself or herself but was allowed to bring friends as *paracletoi* to influence the court by their moral support and witness to his or her moral values as a citizen.[49]

There are several roles of the Paraclete for the sinned-against in the New Testament. First, *parakletos* (in a passive form, *parakalein*) means, "one called alongside to help": *para* (to the side of) and *kalein* (to call). This indicates a defense lawyer or an advocate. The role of the Holy Spirit is that of a defender of the disciples for the Synoptic Gospel authors (Matt. 10:20; Acts 6:10). That is not the Johannine case. In a Jewish court, the judge interrogates the defense. So the role of the defense lawyer in a Jewish court is to provide witnessing for the defense: "When the Advocate comes, whom I will send to you from the Father, the Spirit of truth who comes from the Father, he will testify on my behalf" (John 15:26). The Paraclete testifies on behalf of Jesus. Thus, the Paraclete plays the role of a witness for the defense.[50]

Second, *parakletos* (in an active form, reflecting *parakalein*) means "'to intercede, entreat, or appeal to,' thus an intercessor, a mediator, or a spokesperson." This role of intercessor is clear in 1 John 2:1, but in the Gospel of John, the Paraclete speaks through the disciples (15:26–27) in defense of the absent Jesus. The Paraclete in this context can be "helper, friend."[51]

Third, *parakletos* (in an active sense, reflecting *parakalein*) signifies "comfort," thus a comforter or counselor. Although no passage directly mentions the Paraclete's consoling the disciples, the aspect of consolation is implied in the context such as in Jesus' farewell speech that saddens his disciples (John 16:6–7).[52]

Fourth, *parakletos* (as related to *paraklesis*) is used to describe encouragement or exhortation embedded in the preaching of the apostles' witnesses (1 Thess. 3:2; Rom. 12:8; Acts 13:15; Heb. 13:22).[53] Acts reports that the church grew in the encouragement or comfort (*paraklesis*) of the Holy Spirit in spite of the persecution (Acts 9:31).

Fifth, the Paraclete teaches believers everything and reminds them of all that Jesus said to them (John 14:26).

The *Paraclete* plays the role of a defense lawyer, intercessor, comforter, encourager, and teacher, guiding and helping disciples in time of trials and troubles. The resurrected Jesus does not rest but continues his work of liberation, consoling, and healing through the Paraclete.

The Work of the Paraclete

The work of the Paraclete as wounded healer is to comfort the comfortless, to advocate for the rights of victims, to uplift the discouraged, to help the helpless, and to teach people about Jesus' instruction. Having been wounded through Jesus' crucifixion, the Holy Spirit knows the depths of unjust suffering and advocates for victims' rights. The Paraclete makes victims well by empowering them also to become wounded healers.

The Paraclete wastes no experience of victims and makes use of their hurts for the healing of others' wounds: "Blessed be . . . the God of all consolation, who consoles us in all our affliction, so that we may be able to console those who are in any affliction with the consolation with which we ourselves are consoled by God. For just as the sufferings of Christ are abundant for us, so also our consolation is abundant through Christ" (2 Cor. 1:3–5). The God who consoles us is the Paraclete. Jesus makes our consolation abundant through the Paraclete.

Here the term "consolation" in Greek is *paraklesis*. It is the same word to describe the work of the Paraclete. This Comforter is able to comfort the afflicted because he experienced the suffering, crucifixion, death, and resurrection with Jesus. The way God comforts us is the way the Holy Spirit undergoes suffering within us. Consoling is the attribute and work of the Paraclete, the crucified one in our suffering.

The Paraclete knows the depth of the wounds of the afflicted (*han*) because of his or her own experience of *han*. Some wounds within us are too deep to detect. Most of us are not fully aware of the wounds to our own soul. The Holy Spirit, the wounded healer, understands the magnitude of our *han*. The Paraclete searches our depths, knows our own unknowable and indescribable hurts of *han*, and heals them in us as we open ourselves to the Paraclete. The Paraclete alone is the Spirit that knows the deep inner groaning of the suffering: "Likewise the Spirit helps us in our weakness; for we do not know how to pray as we ought, but that very Spirit intercedes with sighs too deep for words" (Rom. 8:26). The "sighs too deep for words" are *han*. Such wounds within us are too deep to heal. The Paraclete who experienced the crucifixion and the resurrection with Jesus groans with us and heals us in compassion.

The Paraclete as the extension of Jesus' resurrection has concretized God's healing on earth. The Paraclete walks with victims and uplifts them every day. God's reign through the Paraclete has come in the midst of this world's troubles and tragedies. The Paraclete is the Spirit that is at work in the community.[54]

The Paraclete heals our diseases as well as our illnesses. To Arthur Kleinman, "*Disease* refers to a malfunctioning of biological and/or psychological processes, while the term *illness* refers to the psychosocial experience and meaning of perceived disease. Illness includes secondary personal and social responses to the primary malfunctioning (disease) in the individual's physiological or psychological status (or both)."[55] Jesus in the form of the Paraclete heals both diseases of the sick and illnesses of wounded people and communities. Inclusive healing takes place at the four levels in the Paraclete : the body (*soma*), the mind (*psyche*), the spirit (*pneuma*), and community. Thus, a new humanity has dawned with the arrival of the Paraclete.

JESUS' CROSS FOR THE RESTORATION OF VICTIMS' DIGNITY: AN ANTI-RETRIBUTION THEOLOGY

Jesus' cross restores victims' integrity and dignity by repudiating the idea of a sin-punishment formula. Such a retribution theology can be found particularly in Deuteronomy and throughout the books of Joshua through 2 Kings, and also in Jeremiah, the twelve Minor Prophets, and a number of Psalms. In brief, this theology holds that obedience to God's law results in a happy, long life, whereas unfaithfulness and sinfulness lead to misery, suffering, illness, poverty, and untimely death.[56]

This theology of retribution was deeply rooted in the hearts of Jews at the time of Jesus. The book of Job was written to protest against such a repressive and retributive theology, which hurts guiltless victims.[57] The book advocates on behalf of the victims of diverse forms of suffering, showing that the nonsinner may suffer from the tragic aspects of life.

Jesus' suffering and death were interpreted by his contemporary Jews as the chastisement of God. Their thinking derived from Scriptures: "His corpse must not remain all night upon the tree; you shall bury him that same day, for anyone hung on a tree is under God's curse. You must not defile the land that the LORD your God is giving you for possession." (Deut 21:23). To them, the Messiah could not suffer, or be crucified; since Jesus had been hung on a tree, he might have been a false messiah cursed by God.

Representing Job in the New Testament, Jesus restored the dignity of those who underwent shame and condemnation. He shared their suffering, shame, and vulnerability, diametrically opposing retribution theology. His suffering and death made it clear that victims of violence are not all sinners or the cursed.

Later some theologians adopted this retributive idea in interpreting Jesus' suffering. Their satisfaction and penal substitution atonement theories subscribe to the sin-punishment formula of a retribution theology—since humans had sinned, someone should have paid for it. According to these theories, Jesus came and died to pay for the sins of other human beings.

Contrary to these atonement theories, Jesus' death repudiates this theology of retribution. God is merciful and forgiving. Even before Jesus' death, God remitted the Israelites' sins when they turned around: "The sacrifice acceptable to God is a broken spirit; a broken and contrite heart, O God, you will not despise" (Ps. 51:17). God forgives the sin of the lost without seeking any bloody sacrifices as they turn away from their sins. It was not because the sins of Israel and the rest of the world were so enormous that Jesus had to come into the world to propitiate God by his death, but because he aspired to transform the world of injustice and violence through his life of truth, justice, and love, he laid down his life for the cause unto death.

Unlike retribution theology, Jesus says aloud on the cross that even an innocent person may experience the forsakenness of God. His untimely death releases victims from the pressure of double pain: the pain of suffering itself and the pain of theological condemnation. His death shows that even the Messiah suffers from human sin, prejudice, violence, and wickedness.

Jesus' blood was not shed to pay human debts to God; rather, it was shed to restore the integrity of victims through God's justice and compassion. Jesus came not to appease God's wrath but to manifest God's intention to restore humanity. His blood demonstrates that even God's chosen one suffered, was put to shame, and was victimized. Contrary to the sin-punishment principle, Jesus came to vindicate suffering victims and to restore their human dignity.

THE MEANING OF LIBERATION

Liberation means to be free from religious, economic, social, political, and cultural domination, injustice, and violence. Liberation has three levels: individual, collective, and structural. At the individual level, it is the deliverance from personal abuse, domination, bondage, or exploitation that is often connected to collective and structural oppression. At the collective level, liberation is the freedom from the oppressive communal customs and traditions that dominate social relations. It is the release from the collective unconscious of injustice, the ethos of cultural dominance, a communal superiority complex, and exclusive ethnocentrism. At the structural level, liberation is the freedom from slavish systems, legitimate racialism, systemic patriarchy, exploitative capitalism, and undemocratic hierarchy.

Liberation is incomplete if the captive is merely freed from something. Only when the captive is liberated into a new relationship of freedom will liberation be achieved. Christians can experience true liberation only in relation to God, the marks of which may be peace, gladness, and freedom. These marks indicate healthy healing after the initial liberation.

Liberation can be achieved by the symbols of Jesus' cross, resurrection, and postresurrection work. Jesus' cross is the symbol of his shared identity with the downtrodden or victims. It is also the symbol of challenge against injustice, principalities, and powers of evil unto death. Jesus' resurrection is the symbol of the hope of victims for the liberation from injustice, principalities, and evil powers. Jesus' postresurrection atoning work through the Paraclete has been clearly displayed in his active participation in victims' healing and liberative processes.

In the preface, I mentioned my rescue from the burning house by my mother. Her rescue corresponds to Jesus' liberation work, not to his salvation work. As a victim, I needed deliverance from the fire and healing from the tragic event; I did not need salvation from my sin as a three-year-old child. Jesus' identification with victims unto death is comparable with my mother's rushing into the fire. The symbols of Jesus' blood, resurrection, and postresurrection work continuously operate to bring forth the abundant life of victims even after their liberation.

Jesus' Atonement for Sinners and Oppressors

In the previous section, we examined the work of Jesus and the Paraclete for the liberation of victims or the sinned-against. In this section, we will consider the work of Jesus and the Paraclete for sinners' salvation.

Jesus did not come to die on the cross. He declared his mission on earth: "The Spirit of the Lord is upon me, because he has anointed me to bring good news to the poor. He has sent me to proclaim release to the captives and recovery of sight to the blind, to let the oppressed go free, to proclaim the year of the Lord's favor" (Luke 4:18–19). To shed his blood was not the aim of Jesus' redemptive work as seen in his mission statement. Any atonement theory that excludes Jesus' work through his proclaiming, healing, teaching, and liberating is incomplete.

Nevertheless, his death brought forth his new life in God—the resurrection and the arrival of the Paraclete. His resurrection continues his salvific work for offenders in the form of the Paraclete. The Paraclete has done the actual work of salvation by transforming people and the world for the past two thousand years.

Facing his imminent execution, Jesus vacillated as to whether he should continue on the course toward death or escape that death. He saw his death as inevitable if he continued his way of confronting the wrong of the authorities. He decided not to escape his death in order to challenge the injustice and evil of the world, unswervingly staying the course.

Jesus knew that he was limited in his physical ministry, but he was aware of the fact that his death would achieve something greater than his physical ministry could do. He promised the arrival of the Advocate beyond the horizon of history to carry on his work of liberation and salvation.

Jesus' blood does basically several things for sinners. First, his death inevitably causes the resurrection and makes the arrival of the Paraclete possible. Second, his blood exposes the violence and injustice of oppressors. Third, his blood reflects the sin and wickedness of sinners and oppressors through the Paraclete. Fourth, his blood declares forgiveness and justification or salvation by faith to the penitent.

THE CROSS AS THE EXPOSURE OF SIN, VIOLENCE, AND EVIL

Like Abel's, Jesus' blood exposes the wrong and violence of evildoers. After Abel was murdered, his blood cried out to God from the ground (Gen. 4:10). Abel's blood cried for the exposure of his brother's crime. By crying out to God, his blood compelled Cain to acknowledge his own crime. Exposed, Cain came to acknowledge what he had done as he asked for God's leniency (4:14).

The cross of Jesus symbolizes God's confrontation with sinners. His blood is not silent but incessantly cries out from the ground. Even after his resurrection, his spilled blood on the ground issues its shrill voice for justice. It cries not for vengeance but for vindication, exposing the violence, injustice, and evil of violators to God and to the world.

His cross directs the attention of wrongdoers to the suffering of victims. The blood and the Paraclete work together to convict wrongdoers of their sins. Jesus' blood is the visible symbol with which the invisible Paraclete confronts sinners or wrongdoers with their need to change.

An insignificant execution of a Jewish carpenter in the first-century Roman Empire has exposed the injustices and evil of all oppressors to God and to the whole world. Jesus' crucifixion is replayed through the starvation of children in Africa, the agony of war victims in Iraq and Afghanistan, tortured prisoners in dark and forgotten prison cells, the victims of ethnic cleansing in the world, exploited young laborers in sweatshops, and numerous abused children and women. Jesus cries out from the cross to protest against torture, murder, exploitation, violence, injustice, and wickedness in the world.

Jesus' blood did not culminate his redemptive work. His resurrection continues his salvific work of challenging offenders in the form of the Paraclete.

The Paraclete is the Spirit of truth (John 14:17; 15:26; 16:13; 1 John 4:6; 5:6) for oppressors. The Paraclete as the Spirit of truth does several things. First, the Paraclete plays the role of a prosecuting attorney, indicting the world for its wrong. After Jesus' execution and resurrection the Paraclete reminds Jesus' disciples of what he taught them and has taught the world about its wrong understandings. Second, the Paraclete saves them by helping them confess their sins and change their hearts. Third, the Paraclete converts them to do the work of healing victims and establishing God's reign.

THE CROSS AS THE CORRECTION OF THEOLOGICAL IDEAS

The Johannine author announces that when the Paraclete comes, "he will prove the world wrong about sin and righteousness and judgment: about sin, because they do not believe in me; about righteousness, because I am going to the Father and you will see me no longer; about judgment, because the ruler of this world has been condemned" (John 16:8–11). Through the Paraclete, the cross of Jesus corrects people's wrong theological understanding of sin, righteousness, and judgment.

Sin

The Spirit of truth convinces us of the sin that really obstructs God's reign. Unbelief is a primary sin in John (8:24).[58] We usually focus on personal sins, but the Paraclete rectifies this unbalanced idea of sin. Sin has at least three levels: individual, collective, and structural. At the individual level, sin denotes sitting on a controller's throne. It appears as self-grandiosity, selfishness, greed, abusiveness, domination, oppression, exploitation, and lust.[59] At the collective level, sin is the communal customs and traditions that seek the exclusiveness of a group and the collective will-to-power. It is collective conscious and unconscious injustice, wrong, and aggression, the ethos of cultural dominance, a racial superiority complex, exclusive ethnocentrism, and nationalism. At the structural level, sin is the systemic plot against God's providence and reign. In Walter Rauschenbusch's description, "Beyond the feeble and short-lived individual towers the social group as upper-personal entity, dominating the individual, assimilating him to its moral standards, and enforcing them by the social sanctions of approval or disapproval."[60] It is ungodly "composite personalities" that control individuals, corporations, and other organizations. These appear as monopolistic capitalism, racialism, perpetual patriarchy, and undue hierarchy.

The Paraclete convicts people of their sins and wrongs at all three levels—the personal, the collective, and the structural—with conscious and unconscious dimensions. Sin makes people refuse to acknowledge their sinfulness and their need for repentance and forgiveness. The Spirit of truth gently guides sinners to acknowledge their sins and wrongs and leads them to repent of them.

The Spirit of truth changes people's misguided concept of sin. At the time of Jesus, people considered the violations of Sabbath and purity laws as sins. To the Pharisees and scribes, all those who violated such laws were sinners.

The primary reason of Jesus' coming into the world was to bring good news to the afflicted and the sinned-against. Jesus said, "Those who are well have no need of a physician, but those who are sick; I have come to call not the righteous but sinners" (Mark 2:17). Here "sinners" are not all sinners.

There were two types of sinners in Jewish society at that time. One was a publicly recognized violator of civil laws. The other was a person in a lowly and socially unacceptable occupation.[61] We can differentiate the latter type of sinner into two categories. One is comprised of the sinners of dishonorable occupation. The other is comprised of the sinners of low status, such as the sick or the poor. Jesus' followers in general were the disreputable, the uneducated, and the ignorant, whose religious ignorance and moral behavior were obstacles to their access to salvation, according to the public view of the time.[62] They were publicans and sinners (Mark 2:16), prostitutes (Matt. 21:32), or the sick (Luke 5:31). They were simply called "sinners" (Mark 2:17; Luke 7:37, 39).

The sinners of the first category were involved in despised occupations. Some examples were shepherds, tax collectors, and publicans.[63] For instance, shepherds could not observe the Sabbath. These daily laborers had to tend their flocks for their own survival, including on the Sabbath. Others were sinners because of the unclean or ill-smelling nature of their jobs (e.g., dung collectors, tanners, copper smelters). They were alienated and could not partake in worship.[64]

The sinners of the second category were the sick who could not fulfill the duties of the law. As we have seen in Job, the theology that treated sickness as the consequence of sin was widespread in Judaism (Ps. 73; John 9; Mark 2:5). The blind, the lepers, the mentally disturbed, and the hemorrhagic were particularly regarded as either unclean or cursed by God.[65] The sick were not transgressors, but those who suffered under religious legalism.

Most poor and powerless people were called "sinners" by the religious leaders because poverty prevented them from observing the Sabbath or the law of purification. The 'am ha'areṣ were the uneducated and the ignorant, whose lack of religious knowledge and moral practice stood in the way of their entrée to salvation according to the convictions of the time.[66] During the Babylonian exile, the cream of society was taken captive; the common people, including the Samaritans, were left behind. These people were called the 'am ha'areṣ, the people of the land. From the time of Ezra, the term was used to designate a low class of people who were ignorant of the law. Rabbinic

Judaism used the term to refer to the poor and the powerless, who were despised and marginalized.[67]

Jesus came into the world to take their infirmities and bear their grief (cf. Matt. 8:17). He had compassion for the crowds "because they were harassed and helpless" (Matt. 9:36). His proclamation was good news for the *han*-ridden. In Jesus' eyes, the "righteous" were the actual sinners who had to repent of their sin of self-righteousness, religious persecution, and hypocrisy. In contrast to the religious leaders and scribes, Jesus invited the *han*-ridden—the despised, the sick, and the poor— to his rest: "Come to me, all you that are weary and are carry- ing heavy burdens, and I will give you rest" (Matt. 11:28). Their burden was double: public contempt and the hopeless- ness of attaining God's salvation.[68] They were not in fact sin- ners, but were sinned against by the oppressive religious leaders and their legal system.

Jesus tried to rectify this wrong concept of "sinners" by sid- ing with its victims: "Go and learn what this means, 'I desire mercy, not sacrifice.' For I have come to call not the righteous but sinners" (Matt. 9:13). The Paraclete repudiates the sin of unbelief that ignores and rejects Jesus' mission for victims.

The Spirit of truth has continued Jesus' work to confront the misleading sins of the world that oppose God's reign. Recently, we have overemphasized sexual sins and have obscured other important social, political, economic, and global sins such as war, corporate greed, economic and ecological exploitation, white crime, the corrupt influence of lobbyists, and national- ism. For James Cone, racism is the original sin of America. Against the emphases on the internalization and individualiza- tion of sin, the Spirit of truth nudges us to see social alienation (Justo González), the public addiction to consumerism, colo- nialism, militarism, and sexism (Ched Myers), the horizontal sin of violation of the fellow creature, class exploitation and neocolonial exploitation, the humiliation of the vulnerable (Ted Jennings), and harm done to others (Walter Brueggemann).[69] The Paraclete rectifies the one-sidedness of the present under- standing of sin.

Righteousness or Justice

Concerning the term *righteousness*, it is from the Greek noun *dikaiosunē*, which may be translated as either *justice* or *righteousness*. The term *dikaiosunē* is almost always translated *justice* instead of *righteousness* in Greek literature from antiquity, while the New Testament almost never translates it so.[70] While *righteousness* connotes individual piety, *justice* signifies social holiness.[71] The word *basileia* means "dominion, rule, reign, royal power, or kingship." It must not be confused with a concrete kingdom but rather the right or authority to rule over a kingdom.[72] Even though people pursue private righteousness and holiness, the Paraclete teaches us clearly that we need to strive first for God's reign (*basileia*) and God's justice: "See first God's Reign and God's Justice" (Matt. 6:33, au. trans.).

Jesus was executed because people violated God's justice. Violating God's justice is an act of violence. The cross symbolizes the violation of God's justice. That is, the cross is the emblem of violence done against God and the powerless. The Paraclete restores God's justice through the symbol of Jesus' cross.

The justice of God reverses the standards of regular social orders and values (Luke 3:11, 14; 6:20–26). Jesus did not elevate private holiness first, but embodied God's justice and God's reign on earth. The Paraclete has a specific mission to convince people to seek God's justice in order to embody God's reign in the world. God's justice is fair, merciful, and caring, reaching out even to the realms of animals and nature.

Justice means to seek the equity of ethnicity, class, and gender relations and to resist an excessive concentration of wealth; widespread poverty; the reduction of civil, political, and human rights; unilateralist, preemptive wars; and the torture of prisoners. It is to reexamine the widening net of incarceration, revised affirmative action, reduced environmental regulations, and a globalized transnational economy. To bring down God's reign on earth, the Paraclete as a transformative agent gets involved in the peaceful and nonviolent ways of the change of unjust national and global structures and systems.

Judgment

Concerning judgment, the Paraclete will show it by casting out the ruler of this world. Against the prince of this world, a great deceiver and destroyer, such judgment was done through the event of Christ. For George Johnston, "There is a profound sense in which the Devil has been condemned already."[73] The Paraclete breaks the backbone of evil, disarms the power of the destroyer, and introduces a new era of reformation and regeneration.

For Bultmann, this judgment is not a cosmic event in a more distant future, but the "eschatological judgment."[74] The rulers of this world desire to accumulate more power—military power, economic power, political power, and religious power. They believe that power means to control and subjugate those under them. The Paraclete judges their criteria of values, rejects their insatiable hunger for abusive power, and invites them to turn away from their wrongs. The judgment of the Paraclete is to refuse their rejection of truth. For Paul Tillich, God's judgment is "not the negation of love but the negation of the negation of love."[75]

At the same time, Jesus' cross judges offenders abusing others and themselves. By abusing the defenseless, the oppressors dehumanize themselves. By killing others, killers dehumanize themselves first. Jesus humanizes them by putting the brakes on their further evil work. He protests against the practices of evildoers unto death, rejecting their violence and cruelty. He prohibits them from doing evil so that they may come to their senses. His cross signifies God's ultimate stop sign, which serves to save their lives as well as those of the victims.

His blood shows God's rejection of evil while exposing the bloody hands of evildoers. On the cross, he rejects their negation of God's justice. His death is a death to threats of death by the power of evil.

Jesus' blood is evidence of his strong disapproval of their evil, and at the same time of his affirmation of their humanity. Sinners were accepted by Jesus even before they asked for acceptance. Jesus expressed God's tenacious care unto death by confronting them so that God's truth might transform them and allow them to follow the way of God. Jesus' blood is the authority of God that remolds and remakes offenders anew. His cross exposes offenders' evil to restore their lost humanity.

Jesus' cross is the most profound mirror to reflect injustice and evil. God could have used thunderstorms to threaten sinners, but these might have been ineffective in changing their hearts. God could have twisted sinners' arms to make them stop doing evil. Instead, Jesus' way of facing the sinful is the nonviolent way of confrontation that ends the vicious cycle of retribution. Jesus' blood is the most challenging way for God's judgment to speak to and protest against the violence of the unjust. The Paraclete judges the unjust through the way of the cross and the resurrection.

THE CROSS AS THE CHALLENGE TO REPENT

Jesus cannot simply save people by dying for them unless they repent of their sins. He opened a door of repentance for them to come in and to be redeemed. He was executed in the midst of making them turn away from their sins to God by inviting them to the house of salvation. The essential part of his redeeming work for oppressors is to transform them. Jesus' first proclamation was on repentance: "The time is fulfilled, and the kingdom of God has come near; repent, and believe in the good news" (Mark 1:15). His main mission focused on calling people to repentance in preparation for God's reign. Without the actuality of repentance, his redeeming work is only nominal. Challenge or confrontation was his method to turn people away from their sins and wrongs. His cross denotes his challenge unto death to sinners or wrongdoers for their repentance.

Jesus' blood was the strongest protest against evildoers' sins or evil actions, demanding their repentance, recompense, and work for justice. The importance of repentance can be hardly overemphasized for sinners' salvation. The success of Jesus' redemptive work hinges on sinners' repentance.

In fact, all the atonement theories are pointless unless sinners repent of their sins. The ransom theory regards Jesus as our ransom to release us from the bondage of Satan. Although Jesus frees us from being Satan's hostage, we will be chained to sin again if we are unrepentant of our sins. The Christus Victor theory depicts Jesus as the victor in the battle against the cosmic forces of the devil. If sinners remain in their sin, Christ's cosmic victory over the power of Satan is empty. The nonviolent Christus Victor theory faces a similar issue. Christ's nonviolent victory will turn into a defeat if sinners do not repent. The satisfaction theory emphasizes Jesus as God-Man who satisfied the demand of God for the restoration of justice for the offense of sinful humanity against God. If sinners dishonor God again by committing sin, God needs another satisfaction. Underlining the importance of repentance, the moral influence theory points out the fact that Jesus came to show us God's love and to be an example for our life of love. If sinners do not respond to God's ardent love through repentance, God needs to send another, stronger examplar to us. The penal substitution theory modifies Jesus' death as the penalty paid to God for our sins. If sinners do not turn away from their sins, Jesus needs to pay a further penalty for their sins. The last scapegoat theory stresses that Jesus came as the last scapegoat to end the violence of the scapegoating mechanism of society. Jesus' death as the last scapegoat will not be the last one if our society does not end its violence through repentance.

All these diverse atonement theories eventually need to lead sinners or society to repentance. The objective redemptive work of Jesus Christ must concur with the subjective repentance of sinners, if they are to be saved. While most atonement theories are metaphorical, repentance is actual.

The Paraclete with the symbol of Jesus' cross convicts sinners and leads them to turn around from their sins. The Paraclete gently guides them to undergo the process of penance. There can be four steps of repentance: (1) contrition, (2) confession, (3) changing one's heart, and (4) transformed lifestyle.[76]

First, the Paraclete will lead a sinner to the repentance that begins with contrition for one's own sin. The Paraclete wakes up sinners' sleeping consciences by nudging them. The cross of Jesus, a strong symbol of challenge, has the power of waking up sinners to their senses. The first step of contrition is to listen to the voice of the Paraclete through victims' voices.

Earnest listening will lead the wrongdoer to genuine contrition. How sincerely one listens to the wounded determines how earnestly she or he will be penitent. While listening to the story of *han*, people often come to understand the pain of the wounded and undergo deep contrition.

Contrition is an inner transformation; it means having the heart of remorse, regret, and sorrow for what one has done. The act of contrition needs to converge with emptying one's own heart. The work of emptying is a deed of humility. In this respect, the soul can be likened to a cup. Into the cup sinners pour their sinful and evil desires. By the grace of God, sinners can empty their sins, evil desires, and guilt. A sure way to empty the cup is to invite the Paraclete into the soul: the Paraclete pushes sin and guilt out of the cup, filling it instead with the Paraclete's own presence. Central to the act of contrition is the decision not to repeat the sin before God.[77]

Second, the Paraclete guides sinners into the steps of confession. Confession is a noticeable process in being forgiven. When they confess their sins to God and to their victims, they are conveying their desire to be right with God and with their victims.

The Paraclete leads sinners to the public or personal confession of sin. The Epistle of James says, "Therefore confess your sins to one another, and pray for one another, so that you may be healed" (5:16). To be forgiven, sinners need to confess their wrongs to their victims. If they have sinned against God, they only need to confess to God. If they have sinned against others, they need to confess to God and to those who were affected by their sin.

Furthermore, when they sin against someone, they are damaging more than their victim. They sin against the victim's family, relatives, friends, and church. Personal sins have their public dimension. Both private and public sins have communal impacts. Therefore, it is necessary to confess sins personally or publicly according to their relevance.

Confession is an uncomfortable move but an effective step toward halting the repetition of sin. Tough as it is to acknowledge and to confess our sins, wrongs, or failures, that is what God requires and what the Paraclete persuades sinners to do: "If we confess our sins, he who is faithful and just will forgive us our sins and cleanse us from all unrighteousness" (1 John 1:9). Confession helps us acknowledge our wrongs or sins in our heart and with our words. Through confession, the Paraclete makes us leave our pride behind and restores our humility before God and our victims.

Third, the Paraclete exhorts sinners to turn from their sins. Repentance means changing one's mind. This is the fruition of contrition. If anyone wants to repent of his or her sin, he or she must turn back from sin.

Two different New Testament terms describe repentance: *metanoia* and *epistrephō*. *Metanoia* means a change of mind or a turning away from one's own sin, and *epistrephō* signifies going back to God.[78] *Metanoia* signifies a Copernican revolution. It is a reverting to God, through whom sinners also turn to their neighbors. In reconciling with God and victims, sinners may reconcile with God by moving from a self-centered life to a God-centered life and by undergoing the process of repentance with victims if the victims are available. *Metanoia* has two levels: divine and human. At the divine level, repentance denotes reverting to God. Jesus' movement was a repentance movement. The Great Commission in Luke declares, "Repentance and forgiveness of sins is to be proclaimed in his name to all nations, beginning from Jerusalem" (24:47). Repentance and forgiveness are two sides of the same coin. Repentance is for sinners, while forgiveness is from God and from sinners' victims. And at sinners' repentance, heaven rejoices (15:7).

Fourth, the Paraclete directs sinners to walk the walk (Prov. 16:9). Repentance does not mean a change of the heart alone.

It requires action. The Paraclete guides our talk with Jesus into our walk with him.

Epistrephō means "to turn [around, back, from], return, converted, turned to, returned, turned about."[79] Although never translated as "repent," it connotes a lifestyle transformed on the basis of the change in perspective and intention achieved by *metanoia*: "Bear fruits worthy of repentance" (Luke 3:8). Luke uses this term in Acts 26:20: ". . . also to the Gentiles, that they should repent and turn to God and do deeds consistent with repentance." It is a far-reaching transformation under the inspiration of the Paraclete. As in Acts 11:21 and 26:20, this term includes conversion and surrender of the life to God/Christ in faith and a fundamental change in life. Without a converted life, *metanoia* would not be authentic repentance. In the Paraclete, *metanoia* and *epistrephō* occur one after the other. Changing one's behavior includes performing acts of recompense, asking forgiveness from the victim, and seeking reconciliation if the victim wills it.

THE CROSS FOR FORGIVENESS

Regarding Christ's atonement, a pivotal question is this: Does God forgive us without any punishment? In the Hebrew Bible, there are two ways of interpreting God's action in history. The "sin-punishment" formula defends the idea that every sin before its forgiveness must be purified and deterred through punishment. If sin is not punished, God's justice is not served. Human suffering is basically caused by God's punishment. The "sin-forgiveness" formula holds to the idea that God forgives sin without punishing us or remembering it if we repent. God's justice (*mishpat*) is God's mercy. For Walter Brueggemann, God's love is abundant even for transgressors. To him, God is much more compassionate and gracious to their victims! Brueggemann implies that humanity is, after all, a victim of the cosmic drama of creation and the fall. That the God of the Hebrew Bible is a God of mercy and grace is the foundation of the Old

Testament theology. In contrast with the popular mechanistic image of God in the theology of retribution, Brueggemann cogently brings out the compassionate and generous image of God, who allows Job's questions about God's own justice and goodness concerning the problem of evil.[80]

In the Gospels, God forgives people with no punishment when they repent of their sins. In Jesus' parable of the Lost Son (Luke 15), the father unconditionally forgives the second son. Even though he suffered while the son was lost, there is no punishment upon his return. Instead, he celebrates the son's return.

Jesus also taught us how to forgive our offenders. We must forgive them seventy times seven times (Matt. 18:22). It was the Jewish custom to forgive offenders up to three times, but Jesus taught us to forgive our offenders without limit. He mentioned no punishment in the practice of forgiveness. Jesus himself taught a much more graceful practice of forgiveness than the generous Jewish custom of forgiveness. Would God not forgive sinners seventy times seven?

If God forgave people before the event of the crucifixion, what is the purpose of his work?[81] Jesus did not come and die to limit the horizon of forgiveness but rather to open it more widely through his work.

If this is the case, the satisfaction and substitution theories have a problem. The sin-punishment formula is thoroughly operating in them. If God forgives us after punishing Jesus, this is not forgiveness. This is an act of retribution. Some people say that God cannot just forgive sinners without punishment because of God's justice. Does unconditional forgiveness go against God's justice?

As we reviewed above, God has forgiven sinners without any condition when they repented of their sins. God speaks through Isaiah, "Come now, let us argue it out, says the LORD: though your sins are like scarlet, they shall be like snow; though they are red like crimson, they shall become like wool" (Isa. 1:18). God's justice is forgiveness! The true justice of God is the mercy of God that does not impose a punishment upon a sinner but restores a broken relationship.

Jesus never shed his blood because of God's punishment, but he shed his blood to death to challenge sinners to turn away from their sins and to live the life of salvation. Even now he bleeds in the sense that Jesus never gives up his endeavor to save sinners from their sins in spite of their rejection of him. His cross exhibits God's ardent desire for turning sinners around and God's mercy toward repenting sinners.

His core teaching on salvation is revealed in the parable of the Lost Son. The parable debunks any image of God as a purveyor of "sin-punishment." In the parable, the son has the courage to decide to go home in the belief that his father will at least hire him as one of his servants. He gets up and returns home—it is the act of repentance. It is very clear that the returning son is saved by the father's compassion through the son's faith with the act of repentance, not through any blood. Jesus did not demand any blood for the salvation of sinners, contrary to popular literal interpretations of some biblical verses. His teaching on salvation obviously does not include demanding his own blood because Jesus could not teach salvation by his own literal blood before his own death. The fact that Jesus saved many people during his lifetime negates the absolute necessity of his blood for our salvation.

The following passages, however, clearly say something else about the atonement by blood: "For, as life, it is the blood that makes atonement" (Lev. 17:11) and "Without the shedding of blood there is no forgiveness of sins" (Heb. 9:22). The author of Hebrews echoes a common rabbinic theme by saying this.[82] Upholding the idea that Jesus' death inaugurates the new covenant as a covenant sacrifice, the author mainly shows that the new covenant replaces the old covenant. Ironically, the author points out that Christ is the end of the rituals of sacrifice. C. M. Tuckett explains: "Thus the whole argument of Hebrews, which is so clearly indebted to sacrificial categories, ends up by being almost anti-sacrificial in its insistence on the finality of Christ's saving work."[83]

Thus, this passage and the one from Leviticus need to be interpreted from their historical contexts of the priestly tradition,

which regarded animal sacrifices as the requirement for the obser-
vation of the law of Moses. After the destruction of the temple in
70 CE, the Israelites could not offer any sacrifices but had to seek
forgiveness through an alternative way—repentance alone. Yom
Kippur (the Day of Atonement, Lev 23:27–28) after 70 CE has
been the most sacred holy day of fasting and prayer for the forgiveness of sins committed during the year, although this holy
day in ancient times required animal sacrifices in the temple.

What God really stresses is a penitent heart for the forgiveness of sin, not just blood: "The sacrifice acceptable to God is
a broken spirit; a broken and contrite heart, O God, you will
not despise" (Ps. 51:17). God forgives sin as we come to God
with a broken heart.

Forgiveness through repentance is the core of Jesus' teaching
in contrast to ritualistic teaching on atonement through animal
sacrifices. In the parable of the Lost Son, the older son opposes
the father's acceptance and forgiveness of the sinful brother in
the absence of proper observances of the law.

The story of Zacchaeus (Luke 19:1–10) is an actual account
of a lost son. The Pharisees grumbled that Jesus associated with
such a sinner. Zacchaeus made a critical decision to give half of
his possessions to the poor and to recompense generously those
he defrauded. He decided to go far beyond the requirements of
legal demands for fraud in his act of restitution. Seeing in Zacchaeus such a heart of repentance, Jesus accepted him, forgave
him, and declared his salvation: "Then Jesus said to him,
'Today salvation has come to this house, because he too is a son
of Abraham'" (19:9).

Zacchaeus was forgiven and saved even before Jesus shed his
blood.[84] His repentance was sufficient for him to be saved.
Jesus himself never required his own blood to save people. Jesus
emphasized forgiveness through repentance rather than rituals
or observances of the laws for salvation.

If God can forgive sins and save sinners without shedding
the blood of Jesus, why did Jesus shed his precious blood? Jesus
did not shed his blood *for* his afflicters, torturers, and wrong-

doers, but he shed his blood *because* of them. They afflicted, tortured, and executed him. Jesus protested against the injustice, exploitation, and oppression of the rulers and the social structures of his day; consequently, he was executed. His death represents God's suffering for the transformation of the oppressors as well as unjust and evil social structures. His execution also represents the suffering and executions of social transformers for the sake of establishing God's reign. We may, however, say that Jesus died for the sins of sinners or oppressors in the following sense: Jesus resisted and challenged his persecutors and oppressors unto death so that they might come to their senses and be saved.

As Jesus forgave his persecutors and murderers, Jesus' blood symbolizes the forgiveness that transcends the habits of the human mind. This fact allows us to say that his blood is divine. Jesus' blood contained no more red and white blood cells than that of any other person. He was a truly human being, with a typical human body. When he was tired, he rested. When he was sad, he wept. When he was whipped, he bled and felt pain.

The divine dimension of his blood does not mean that his blood was supernatural. His blood was normal human blood. His blood type was one of the following: A, B, AB, or O. There was no divine blood mingled with the human in his system. God has no blood, but Jesus' blood had its divine dimension— the courage to challenge, to forgive, and to care. There is no power greater than God's care for creation. What saves us does not flow from the penalty Jesus suffered, the victory he won, or the ransom he paid for us, but from the ardent care of God. The divine care became flesh and dwelt among us as a friend, not as an enemy. "No one has greater love than this, to lay down one's life for one's friends" (John 15:13), or even for one's opponents (Rom. 5:8). It is not Jesus' biological blood itself that saves us, but God's challenging care.

Here is an inspirational story of forgiveness. Rev. Yang-Won Son (1902–1950) was a remarkable Christian. He served a Presbyterian congregation in Yuhsu, a southern port city in

Korea. Almost all his ministry revolved around care for the residents of leper colonies. Under the Japanese occupation (1910–1945), he refused to pay homage to the Japanese emperor at the Shinto shrine, and the Japanese police sent him to an island leprosarium to break his rebelliousness. After three years the unrepentant pastor returned home. Three years after Korea regained its independence in 1945, the communist revolt took place in Yuhsu. Son's two teenaged sons, Tong-In Son and Tong-Sun Son, were shot to death by a rebel youth when they refused to renounce their faith. Instead of being swept by hatred and retaliation, Rev. Son forgave the shooter in the name of Jesus, saved him from a death sentence by petitioning for his release, and adopted him as his son. Moved by the genuine forgiving love of Rev. Son, the adopted youth truly repented his unspeakable crime and strived to fulfill all of the pastor's expectations toward him. Rev. Son gave him all the love and guidance that he had provided to Tong-In and Tong-Sun. He became a devout Christian and a good student. This story of forgiveness spread throughout Korea. During the Korean War, the North Korean troops took both of them as hostages and executed them before their retreat in August 1950.[85]

The ripple effects of Jesus' forgiveness have been enormous, transforming the culture of fatalism, nihilism, unforgiving spirit, bitterness, and the survival of the fittest into the culture of self-determinism, care, forgiveness, and gracefulness. It is with Jesus that the genuine forgiveness movement started in history. After Christ's death, his followers began to forgive their offenders in the name of Jesus. The Judaism of Jesus' day stressed the legalistic interpretations of the law over grace and forgiveness. While no major religions underscore forgiveness, Jesus taught forgiveness as a major theme of his message and pronounced unlimited forgiveness, elevating the level of human consciousness to a higher plane of graciousness— a divine level. Jesus embodied his teaching of forgiveness toward his wrongdoers or persecutors from the high position of the cross.

JESUS' CROSS FOR JUSTIFICATION BY FAITH

How is the blood of Jesus connected to our understanding of justification by faith? We usually separate the doctrine of justification from Jesus' atonement. As a matter of fact, they point to the same reality—salvation by grace.

Sinners are justified by faith alone. Faith means to accept God's unconditional forgiveness and acceptance. Justification by faith transpires when the sinners or oppressors accept the fact that Jesus, who represents their victims, died on the cross *because of* their sin and that they need to turn away from sin and to turn to God and their victims.

The Epistle to the Ephesians proclaims our salvation by faith alone: "For by grace you have been saved through faith, and this is not your own doing; it is the gift of God" (Eph. 2:8). Salvation is not achieved by our piety but by the pure grace of God. Not even because Jesus shed his blood does God save us. But because God is utterly gracious, God saves us.

Jesus taught God's gracious forgiveness and practiced that forgiveness throughout his ministry. The cross of Jesus highlights God's forgiving heart toward sinners or oppressors. Accepting this unconditional forgiving grace of God is faith. God's salvation does not hinge upon any sacrifice or our devoutness, but on God's grace alone. Salvation is God's gift, not derived from any fixed formula, including blood sacrifice. Faith, accepting God's gracious offer of forgiveness, is the only condition we need to be saved. Faith alone, *sola fide*, precedes even the blood of Jesus as the precondition of God's salvation.

The real meaning of faith alone even goes beyond the belief that our faith saves us. God's grace alone saves us! Faith is the courage to accept God's grace and to start a new life.

THE MEANING OF SALVATION

From time to time we hear this question: "Are you saved?" What does it mean to be saved? Numerous people aspire to be

saved. If we ask them the meaning of salvation, they may
answer that salvation means entering heaven after this life. For
some Christians, salvation means relaxing, reposing in heaven,
walking down the golden streets after going through pearly
gates, and attending exquisite banquets day after day. Salvation, however, does not denote entering a certain place. It is not
a Hawaiian vacation. A Hawaiian vacation may become very
boring after a certain period of time. Salvation is much more
meaningful than that.

For the church, salvation means "freedom from the law
and its anxiety-producing and condemning power" (classical
Protestantism), "freedom from death and error" (the early
Greek Orthodox church), "freedom from guilt and its out-
comes in this and the next life" (the Roman Catholic Church),
"the conquest of the godless state through conversion and
regeneration" (Pietism and revivalism), and "the overthrowing
of special sins and progress toward moral perfection" (ascetic
and liberal Protestantism).[86]

Salvation is for sinners. Jesus' blood stands for victims' outcries and God's demand for their repentance. Through the
symbol of Jesus' blood, the Paraclete pronounces God's forgiveness at their repentance.

Salvation should be more than achieving a certain secure
state of life or beyond life. It is more than the freedom from sin
and destruction. The essence of salvation is not to obtain something but to live with God. In other words, it is *our freedom to
choose to be with God*. When we are with God, all other things
become secondary.

More concretely, to be with God is to relate to God. In such
a fellowship with God, we experience God's friendship, illuminating the meaning of our life. In short, salvation is not a possession but a relationship. At a deeper level, it is to enjoy the
abundant life by deepening our love with God. Loving God
more and more transports us to a new height in the meaning of
life, richer and fuller. Wherever and whenever God is with us,
there opens heaven. God's presence generates heaven. Salvation
transpires when we change from a self-centered life to a God-

centered life. Salvation happens now as we accept God as our center. Eternal life, heaven, and freedom from sin and evil are the results of our relationship with God, not vice versa.

Our relationship with God can be severed by nothing, even by death, unless we sever it by ourselves. Salvation continues beyond this life, but what we experience now carries on to the future. In the last century, Rudolf Bultmann, Paul Tillich, and a host of other theologians emphasized this present tense of salvation. They focused on the way God interacts with humans in this very moment of existence.

Salvation is not a futuristic ego trip. As soon as we project heaven as the place where we pick up gold nuggets on golden streets and wear diadems as kings or queens to rule over others, heaven closes down. A paradise with our craving for power, mammon, and reputation is a paradise lost. Plainly, being with God is our heaven in this life and beyond.

Jesus' Atonement for the Han *of Animals and Nature*

Against the idea of dualism that regards matter as evil and spirit as good, both the Hebrew Bible and the New Testament describe how much God cares for the created world. The world created by God is good, and God commissioned humans to take care of it: "The Lord God put the man in the garden of Eden to care for it and work it" (Gen. 2:15 New Century Version). Jesus' work is not only for the redemption of humanity but also for the restoration of the whole creation. He shows that God cares about the well-being of animals and nature.

THE HEBREW BIBLE

The Hebrew Bible contains a progressive knowledge of God concerning nature. The Hebrew Bible is first centered on the event of the deliverance of Israel from Egypt and the covenant of Sinai, affirming the experience of redemption.[87] Its theology of redemption precedes the theology of creation. This is the reason why the book of Exodus was written before the book of Genesis.

The Hebrew Bible, however, gradually interweaves human sins and human redemption with the disruption of nature and its restoration, according to G. W. H. Lampe. He articulates the prophetic and apocalyptic contributions to the Hebraic understanding of nature, noting that its view of the redeemed people of God takes account of a renewal of the whole creation.[88] Although humans alone have the image of God and the ability to take care of nature, they also belong to nature. They are made of dust and go back to dust. Humans have an interdependent relationship with nature.

More concretely, Paul Santmire points out in his book *The Travail of Nature* that the land-blessing theology of the Deuteronomic traditions and the fecundity theology of the Priestly writing and the Psalms run through the backbone of the creation theology in the Hebrew Bible.[89]

On the one hand, the land is considered as a gift in Deuteronomy. For Walter Brueggemann, "Land is a central, if not the central theme of biblical faith."[90] It is an area of great blessing and fertility. God is the owner of the land: "For the land is mine; with me you are but aliens and tenants" (Lev. 25:23). Deuteronomy places the land as great blessing and fertility. This theme is striking in two ways. First, this theme is impressive because its idea is derived from the northern kingdom, where its theological struggle with Baal (the god of nature) was intense. The Deuteronomic tradition and the Elohist tradition are rooted in the northern kingdom and celebrate the land as a divine gift. Second, the fertility of Yahweh's land is a striking theme. This is about divine blessing. Claus Westermann studied this theme and came up with a conclusion: two themes, God's deliverance and God's blessing, are self-consciously connected in the Bible.[91] God's saving is God's blessing.[92]

On the other hand, the poets of Israel praise the multiple fecundity of Yahweh throughout the whole earth. The Priestly writer is conspicuously mindful of God's nature and leads the fecundity theme to reach one of its most impressive expressions in Genesis 1, "a kind of self-conscious architectonic fascination with the earth and its fullness."[93] A number of the psalms, particularly the royal psalms (e.g., 47, 97), highlight Yahweh's universal rule over the earth as Yahweh ascends to the heavenly throne: "The LORD is king! Let the earth rejoice; let the many coastlands be glad!" (Ps. 97:1).

Other descriptions of the fecundity theme express Yahweh's personal attention and care for all creatures, however small and strange they may be. Yahweh knows "all the birds of the air" (Ps. 50:11), "saves humans and animals alike" (Ps. 36:6), gives them "their food in due season" (Ps. 145:15), instructs Noah to "bring two of every kind into the ark, to keep them [animals] alive" (Gen. 6:19), and makes God's covenant with Noah, with his descendants, and with every creature on earth (Gen. 9:10), and calls the stars by name (Isa. 40:26).

Psalm 104 epitomizes the rich expression of the fecundity theme, uniting both the architectonic vision of the Priestly writer (light as God's garment, the heavens as God's tent, and the clouds as God's chariot) and the personalized images of God in the Psalms (giving drink to every beast of the field, growing grass for the cattle, and giving birds their habitation).[94] Furthermore, nature's praise of Yahweh (sun and moon, sea monsters, mountains, and all hills) in Psalm 148 is the indispensable portion of God's joy. The Priestly traditions depict a world of God's glory, beauty, and harmony: "The heavens are telling the glory of God; and the firmament proclaims his handiwork" (Ps. 19:1).[95] Gerhard von Rad holds that the Sabbath signifies the future, the eschatological fulfillment of the whole creation.[96]

In summary, Deuteronomy depicts the land as God's great blessing and fertility, while the Priestly writer and the psalmist celebrate the fecundity of Yahweh over the whole earth. Even in times of despair, the prophets, particularly the apocalyptic ones, proclaimed the promise of a renewed land and earth for Israel often with bountiful images of overflowing fecundity. This can be seen in Second Isaiah from the exilic period. Even if God judged Israel, God would renew the land when Israel repented of its sin. Later, in times of deepest despair when such a renewal of the land and its fecundity for Israel were unrealizable, the emergent literature of the apocalyptic prophets raised an inclusive hope for the whole earth beyond this world—a day of new heavens and new earth.[97] This is true also in the case of Third Isaiah: "For I am about to create new heavens and a new earth; the former things shall not be remembered or come to mind" (65:17). The vision of the apocalyptic writers in the prophetic tradition fully coalesces the two themes of land and fecundity.[98]

THE NEW TESTAMENT

Jesus was apocalyptic in his proclamation. His apocalyptic message points to the renewal of heaven and earth. According to Edward Schillebeeckx, Jesus' vocation was to initiate the last days of the creation in judgment and grace.[99] It is a future expectation of the transformation of heaven and earth. Some forms of apocalyptic theologies were dualistic. Influenced by the gnostic idea that spirit is good and matter is evil, dualistic apocalyptists denied the value of the whole creation. William Manson holds that new heavens and a new earth mean not the destruction of the cosmos but its renovation.[100]

Santmire holds that there are two motifs in the interpretation of the New Testament: the spiritual and the ecological. The spiritual motif refers to the redemption of the fallen rational spirits through the work of Jesus and the eschatological union of humanity with Jesus Christ. It is articulated by the Gospel of John and the Epistle to the Hebrews.[101] Origen read the Scriptures through this spiritual motif by projecting the purpose of all things as the return of the fallen spirits to God for union. St. Thomas, while holding the goodness of creation, affirmed the aim (*telos*) of the whole creation is primarily the beatitude of the saints and the angels alone in heaven with God. Bonaventure, Dante, Teilhard de Chardin, and Karl Barth support this spiritual mode of thinking.[102]

The ecological motif signifies the divine restoration of all creation through the redemption of fallen humanity by the universal reign of Jesus Christ. In this motif, says Santmire, "creation and redemption, redemption and creation, are symmetrical."[103] The ecological motif is the way of thinking that every creature shall enjoy the glorious liberation of God. This motif is seen in the dynamics of Hebraic faith, the apocalyptic proclamation of Jesus, and the apocalyptic theology of Paul and the Pauline authors of Colossians and Ephesians. Irenaeus, the mature Augustine, Francis, and, to a considerable degree, Luther and Calvin read the Scriptures through the ecological motif.[104]

Paul stresses the universal vision of salvation as well as the individual's faith in Jesus Christ: "For from him and through him and to him are all things. To him be the glory forever" (Rom. 11:36). This vision holds that whatever God creates is good and is cared for by God. Toward the last days of the world, we will see God more present in "all in all" (1 Cor. 15:28). *All in all* is the vision of renewal, not the vision of destruction for the world.

These two motifs have coexisted in the Bible. Santmire thinks that a large majority of contemporary Christian scholars choose the spiritual motif of interpretation. He believes that when these scholars take the ecological reading of the Scriptures seriously, "a new birth of Christian thought about nature" will bring forth a blessed ending of the travail of nature.[105]

We need not separate these two motifs. God is our creator and redeemer. By creating the cosmos, God places God's self in relationship with God's creation. God is not an autocrat but a gracious creator who would like to have an "I and Thou," not an "I and It" relationship with God's creation. Jesus is the embodiment of such an "I and Thou" relationship of God with humans and with the whole creation. In Jesus, God meets, saves, and heals fallen and injured humanity and wounded nature. Jesus is the crossroads of the restoration of God's creation and God's redemption and the crossroads of the spiritual and ecological motifs of the Scriptures.

THE HEALING OF THE *HAN*
OF ANIMALS AND NATURE

Beyond human *han* there is the *han* of animals and nature, who suffer from abusive treatment by humans yet are unable to protest against it. They can only groan over their lot. There is no term to describe such a miserable condition of animals and nature. The inexpressible pain of "speechless" animals and nature is *han*. Paul amazingly articulates such a form of *han*:

For the creation waits with eager longing for the revealing of the children of God; for the creation was subjected to futility, not of its own will but by the will of the one who subjected it, in hope that the creation itself will be set free from its bondage to decay and will obtain the freedom of the glory of the children of God. We know that the whole creation has been groaning in labor pains until now; and not only the creation, but we ourselves, who have the first fruits of the Spirit, groan inwardly while we wait for adoption, the redemption of our bodies. (Rom. 8:19–23)

The creation has been forced to serve human whims and has suffered pain in silence. The creation was not meant to be subjected to human exploitation.

Paul was deeply touched by the fact that the whole created order was chained to decay and futility. To John Cobb and David Lull, through these passages of the final salvation Paul shares his vision of the transformation of the faithful on the one side, and of the rest of the creation on the other.[106] For him, human bondage to sin is bound up with the suffering of creation. If human sin causes the suffering and subjugation of creation, there can still be hope, because the final victory over sin will end creation's subjection to futility. To Paul, creation longs eagerly for such liberation.[107]

Paul's vision of Jesus' work is cosmic. He envisions Jesus' being not only for the redemption of humanity but also for the restoration of God's created order. As the children of God, filled with the first fruits of the Spirit, we will participate in the liberation of the creation.

Presently, the whole creation is groaning under sin and *han*. According to a Worldwatch Institute report, we have crossed one threshold—the limit of nature. If we cross a second threshold, there will be an unprecedented and irreversible change in climate.[108] We can still avert that happening. Crossing these thresholds creates nature's *han*. Nature tries to cope with all the stress it has received, but when it is unable to bear the burden any more, it will collapse. That is *han*.

The environmental stress caused by technological advance is so tremendous that we face natural catastrophes. The atmosphere is being irrevocably damaged before our eyes. Each year humanity dumps roughly 8 billion metric tons of carbon into the atmosphere, 6.5 billion tons from fossil fuels used by power plants, cars, automatic machines, furnaces, and other equipment, and 1.5 billion resulting from deforestation. An average resident of the United States contributes up to more than five metric tons of carbon a year.[109] In 2007, the United States produced the most CO_2 from electricity generation, releasing 2.8 billion tons of CO_2, and China was close to surpassing it, with its 2.7 billion tons.[110]

Such human activities are related to global warming, one of the greatest threats to humankind and other species. NASA's Goddard Institute of Space Studies reported that the average global temperature in 2005 was 14.6 degrees Celsius, making it the warmest year ever recorded on Earth's surface. Since record keeping began in 1880, the five warmest years have all taken place since 1998. The average global temperature has risen 0.8 degrees Celsius in the past century. A rise of 0.6 degrees has happened in the past thirty years, and this warming trend is accelerating.[111] National Geographic News reports the following:

> Sea levels could rise between 7 and 23 inches (18 to 59 centimeters) by century's end, according to a February 2007 report by the the United Nations' Intergovernmental Panel on Climate Change (IPCC). A rise of just 4 inches (10 centimeters) could flood many South Seas islands as well as large parts of Southeast Asia.
>
> Some hundred million people live within 3 feet (1 meter) of mean sea level, and much of the world's population is concentrated in vulnerable coastal cities.
>
> Glaciers around the world could melt, causing sea levels to rise while creating water shortages in regions dependent on runoff for fresh water.
>
> Strong hurricanes, droughts, heat waves, wildfires, and other natural disasters may become commonplace in

many parts of the world. The growth of deserts may also cause food shortages in many places.[112]

The IPCC found that the amount of water pouring annually from the ice sheet into the ocean—equivalent to the amount of water the United States uses in three months—caused global sea levels to rise by 3.1 millimeters per year from 1993 to 2003.[113] The Antarctic holds 90 percent of the world's ice, and the disappearance of even its smaller West Antarctic ice sheet could raise worldwide sea levels by an estimated 20 feet.[114]

As governments gathered in 2007 in Bali, Indonesia, to discuss the future of the Kyoto Protocol, the United Nations Development Programme's Human Development Report suggested a "21st Century carbon budget" for staying within the threshold of 2°C (3.6°F) above preindustrial levels (the current level is 0.7°C, 1.3°F), necessitating the forging of a multilateral agreement for the period after 2012, when the Kyoto Protocol is set to expire. The report warns that on current trends the world is more likely to breach a 4°C threshold than stay within 2°C. The report provides evidence of the mechanisms through which the ecological impacts of climate change would be passed on to the poor. Focusing on the 2.6 billion people surviving on less than two U.S. dollars a day, the authors of the report caution that forces let loose by global warming could stall and then reverse the progress achieved over generations.[115] As dramatic climate changes have threatened food supplies, the UN's World Food Programme warns that forty million people in Africa risk starvation due to weather factors, health issues, civil strife, and economic policies.[116]

The worldwide trend is to replace small family farms with "factory farms," where the production of livestock, poultry, and fish is confined and concentrated. Animal factory farming causes a great deal of animal cruelty.

Let's briefly look into animal factory farms. Like cats and dogs, chickens are inquisitive, social, intelligent animals.[117] When I was young, my family raised chickens. We watched how chickens spent their days together, scratching for food, chasing each other, taking dust baths, roosting in tree branches, and sitting in the sun. Unfortunately, chickens raised on factory farms each year never have the chance to do any of those natural things. They never meet or know their parents. They never fully fledge their wings, breathe fresh air, enjoy dust baths, feel sunshine on their backs, roost in a tree, or raise their chicks.

"Broilers," baby chickens overgrown for their flesh, spend their entire lives in filthy shacks with tens of thousands of other birds. To prevent outbreaks of disease from intense crowding and confinement, antibiotics are regularly given. Factory farmers drug them to grow so quickly that their legs and organs are unable to keep up, often causing heart attacks, organ failure, and leg deformities. A number of them become unable or reluctant to move under their own weight, and their claws curl around the wire floor and entrap them. Some even starve to death because they can't reach food or water.[118] Six- or seven-week-old chickens—about 35 million a day in the United States—are crammed into cages and trucked to slaughter.[119]

Pigs are very friendly, loyal, and clever animals.[120] A sow for breeding pigs is confined for most of her life in a pen about two feet by seven feet, and is unable to stand or turn around.[121] Designed for soft soil, her feet are forced to carry hundreds of pounds of weight on concrete, causing severe foot and leg problems. Unable to do any of her natural routines, "the sow goes mad and exhibits compulsive, neurotic 'stereotypical' behaviors such as bar-biting and purposeless chewing."[122] Shortly after giving birth, she is impregnated again and again for years until her body finally gives out and she is sent to be killed.

Her piglets are weaned as early as three weeks. Taken away from their mother, they are then sent to cramped and barren pens without any bedding material, which frustrates their natural desire to root around. These stressful conditions aggravate their aggressive behavior such as tail biting; to prevent this, their tails are cut off. Some of their teeth and the testicles of male pigs are cut off without anesthesia.[123] Overcrowded crates on a tiny slab of filthy concrete are their only homes for their entire lives.

Researchers at the University of Edinburgh created a "pig park" that comes close to the habitat of wild swine. They let loose domestic pigs in this facility and observed their behavior. In this park, the sows covered almost a mile in rooting around and built nests carefully constructed on a hillside so that urine and feces ran downhill. They kept up with their reputation as clean animals. They foraged, and took turns minding each other's piglets. Such natural behavior is inexpressible in confinement.[124]

The billions of animals raised in factory farms have physical and behavioral problems. One of the most glaring cases is confinement of veal calves. Separated from their mothers just days after birth, the calves are caged in a tiny space that impedes them from moving more than a few steps. Naturally gregarious calves are isolated, unable to stretch or lie down comfortably for the entire four months of their lives. Against their normal sucking habits, the calves are fed from buckets, so they neurotically suck and chew their crates.[125] With no pain relievers, male calves' testicles are cut from their scrotums.

Beef cattle are also pumped full of drugs to make them grow faster. Liver abscesses in slaughtered beef cattle result from aggressive grain-feeding programs. Beef cattle get antibiotics on a regular basis to ward off disease. Lots of feedlot owners simply give sick cattle higher doses of antibiotics in an attempt to keep them alive long enough to make it to the slaughterhouse.[126]

The Hebrew Bible forbids us to neglect animals or to cause intentional, deviant, and unnecessary suffering and pain to them: "The righteous know the needs of their animals, but the mercy of the wicked is cruel" (Prov. 12:10). We are commanded not to plow an ox and an ass together because of the hardship to the weaker one (Deut. 22:10). Killing an ox would be like killing a man: "Whoever slaughters an ox is like one who kills a human being" (Isa. 66:3). The injunction against "boiling a kid in its mother's milk" is found in several passages (Exod. 23:19; 34:26; Deut. 14:21). It is forbidden to slaughter an animal along with its young on the same day (Lev. 22:28).

The Hebrew Bible nurtures compassion for animals as a virtue and encourages sensitivity to animal well-being. Psalm

145 declares that God's mercy extends over all creatures: "The LORD is good to all, and his compassion is over all that he has made" (v. 9). God cares for the rest of the animals on the Sabbath when humans rest (Exod. 20:10; 23:12). We are required to help animals: "You shall not see your neighbor's donkey or ox fallen on the road and ignore it; you shall help to lift it up" (Deut. 22:4). Jesus acknowledged to an audience of lawyers and Pharisees that they would save a child or an ox that fell into a well even if they must violate the Sabbath (Luke 14:5).[127]

Confinement agribusiness clearly violates core biblical principles of husbandry and responsible stewardship over the earth. God has not granted an unqualified license to humans to kill or inflict suffering on animals. The dominion of confinement agribusiness pollutes the earth, degrades community, destroys small, independent farmers, and controls our food supply.

Furthermore, overeating meat is costly: "To produce 1 pound of feedlot beef requires about 2,400 gallons of water and 7 pounds of grain. Considering that the average American consumes 97 pounds of beef (and 273 pounds of meat in all) each year, even modest reductions in meat consumption in such a culture would substantially reduce the burden on our natural resources."[128] Paul said that he would never eat meat that was offered to an idol, if that food might cause a weak believer to fall. For him, eating meat in such a case was an act of sin against a fellow believer and thus against Christ (1 Cor. 8:12–13). Is it time for Christians to consider eating less meat and other animal products, if such a decision may help the hungry of the world and alleviate the suffering of farm animals and the burden on the environment?

The International Food Policy Research Institute has reported that in the Philippines, Brazil, and Thailand, small livestock farms may be more efficient than larger production operations at generating profits per unit of output.[129] When mad cow disease broke out in Europe, British scientists blamed it on factory farming methods.[130] German chancellor Gerhard Schroeder called for an end to factory farming in 2000.[131] Some day we will end all inhumane and health-risking factory farming and learn how to live with nature and animals humanely and naturally by attaining our true humaneness.

Acid rain, deforestation, and toxic chemical dumps have polluted, contaminated, and destroyed trees, water, air, and soil. Human actions that contradict the will of nature and animals generate groans in them. Christians have ignored the *han* of animals and nature in the past. Facing ecological disasters, we experience and are affected by their *han*. Their *han* is closely connected to human sin and global disasters. God pronounced, "Cursed is the ground because of you" (Gen. 3:17), when the first humans committed sin.

The story of Cain and Abel (Gen 4:1–16) exposes not only the reality of human sin and *han* but also the *han* of nature. After Cain killed Abel, Abel's blood cried out from the ground. The ground, God's holy ground, was polluted by human blood. Human sins pollute the sacredness of nature and animals. In order to fulfill the holistic vision of God's restoration, the human family needs to remove pollution from nature, dissolving the *han* of animals and nature. The Christian vision of wholeness includes the healing of all God's creation. It is time for us to transcend humanocentrism in our understanding of the cosmic fulfillment of God's creation.

The creation story in Genesis 2 and 3 shows our origin: *Adam* (humankind) is made of *adamah* (dust or soil), tills *adamah* (field), and then goes back to *adamah*. The sequence is *adamah-adam-adamah*. We are of soil. When we sin, the soil is polluted. When soil is polluted, we are polluted too. The earth is not made only for humans. After creating living creatures on the fifth day, God blessed them and declared, "Be fruitful and multiply and fill the waters in the seas, and let birds multiply on the earth" (Gen. 1:22). Furthermore, the Noahic covenant after the great flood made it very clear that God counts animals in the vision of God's restoration: "As for me, I am establishing my covenant with you and your descendants after you, and with every living creature that is with you, the birds, the domestic animals, and every animal of the earth with you, as many as came out of the ark" (Gen. 9:9–10).[132] God's eternal covenant was made not only with the human family but also with every living creature. God gave God's mark of the covenant—the rainbow—to all future generations and the earth (9:12–13). The rainbow is the symbol of God's protection of all generations of humans and animals from destruction by water. Now we ourselves are flooding the earth by melting the polar ice caps, breaking God's covenant of nondestruction by flood. The rainbow symbolizes God's commitment to the well-being of all humans and animals, inviting us to honor God's will.

Like Abel's blood, Jesus' blood cries out from the ground to protest against human violence, human exploitation, and human abuse of fellow human beings, animals, and nature. His death speaks loudly to the futility of animal sacrifices for sinful human beings. His blood cries out from the ground for the restoration of God's sacred creation. "A sabbath of complete rest for the land" points out the sacredness of the ground (Lev. 25:4). Jesus' blood symbolizes the antidote for the ground polluted by human greed and exploitation, reversing the *han* of the ground by extending God's care and love to the whole creation. Jesus' restorative work purifies and detoxifies the polluted and toxic ground by reducing the effect of the poison of infectious human sins. Therefore, Jesus came not only for the salvation and liberation (healing) of humans but also for the realization of the vision of God for the whole creation.

Jesus strives to fulfill the purpose of God's creation. Paul affirms this important task of Jesus Christ: "When all things are subjected to him, then the Son himself will also be subjected to the one who put all things in subjection under him, so that God may be all in all" (1 Cor. 15:28). Until God is all in all, Jesus' re-creative work continues through the Paraclete.

As the Israelites misconstrued their chosenness as God's special favor for them and not as God's special mission of being a light to all the nations (Isa. 49:6), we may mistake the image of God for God's exclusive love for humans alone. Just as chosenness for the Israelites meant their mission to spread God's light and mercy to other nations, so does the image of God in us signify the accountability of human beings to share God's care with other creatures and nature (Gen. 1:28). The New Testament testifies to Christ as the image of God (Col. 1:15; 2 Cor. 4:4). As the image of God, Jesus does not show us a god of tyranny, exploitation, and oppression but reveals to us a God of care, mercy, and compassion for the whole creation who feeds sparrows and clothes the lilies of the field (Matt. 6:25–29). As we grow in understanding the image of God, we will be like Jesus, becoming more caring, more revering, and more loving of God's whole creation.

The cross of Jesus represents the crucified image of God for the sake of God's whole creation. Jesus as the crucified image of God symbolically suffers with the polluted earth and with inhumanely treated animals. Jesus' cross also symbolizes the hope of animals' tomorrow as the rainbow of Noah promises God's blessings upon the descendants of those animals. Jesus is the restoration of God's creation, and his cross points to God's unchanging care for the whole creation. Jesus "died on the cross to make peace with all things and to inaugurate the coming of the New Heavens and the New Earth, and who will finally hand over his rule to God, so that God may be all in all."[133]

To fulfill God's purpose for creation, Jesus calls upon us to work for global healing and wholeness, in which all of God's creations live in respect, harmony, and care, rejoicing in each other's company. Isaiah poetically portrays the state of the restored earth of God:

> The wolf shall live with the lamb,
>   the leopard shall lie down with the kid,
> the calf and the lion and the fatling together,
>   and a little child shall lead them.
> The cow and the bear shall graze,
>   their young shall lie down together;
>   and the lion shall eat straw like the ox.
> The nursing child shall play over the hole of the asp,
>   and the weaned child shall put its hand on the
>   adder's den.

They will not hurt or destroy
   on all my holy mountain;
for the earth will be full of the knowledge of the LORD
   as the waters cover the sea.

                                      (11:6–9)

Here the predators and the victims eat and play together, and the oppressors and the oppressed rest and enjoy each other in God's creation. When we come to live with God's nature in harmony, we will be able to acclaim God with shouts of joy: "Holy, holy, holy is the God of hosts; the whole earth is full of your glory" (Isa 6:3).[134]

Notes

Preface

1. Quoted in Maurice Friedman, *Encounter on the Narrow Ridge: A Life of Martin Buber* (New York: Paragon House, 1991), 293.

Introduction

1. See James Cone, "Strange Fruit: The Cross and the Lynching Tree," 2006 Ingersoll Lecture at Harvard Divinity School, October 19, 2006.

2. Joanne Carlson Brown and Rebecca Parker, "For God So Loved the World?" in *Christianity, Patriarchy and Abuse: A Feminist Critique,* ed. Joanne Carlson Brown and Carole R. Bohn (New York: Pilgrim Press, 1989), 1–30.

3. Rita Nakashima Brock and Rebecca Ann Parker, *Proverbs of Ashes* (Boston: Beacon Press, 2001), 230.

4. Delores Williams, *Sisters in the Wilderness: The Challenge of Womanist God-Talk* (Maryknoll, NY: Orbis Books, 1993).

5. Delores Williams, "Black Women's Surrogacy Experience and the Christian Notion of Redemption," in *Cross Examinations: Readings on the Meaning of the Cross Today,* ed. Marit A. Trelstad (Minneapolis: Fortress Press, 2006), 32.

6. JoAnne Marie Terrell, "Our Mothers' Gardens," in Trelstad, ed., *Cross Examinations,* 49.

7. Andrew Sung Park, *From Hurt to Healing: A Theology of the Wounded* (Nashville: Abingdon Press, 2004).

8. "The thief comes only to steal and kill and destroy. I came that they may have life, and have it abundantly."

9. The abundant life is more than freedom from sin, more than freedom from injuries, more than freedom from oppression and injustice. It is the life that is free to care, help, and love others, fulfilling their gifts from God. The abundant life is the life-living, joy-filled eternity in the

midst of anxiety, fear, injury, injustice, absurdity, and persecution. It is the life with and within the Paraclete and is the life of "eternal now." Jesus saves sinners and liberates their victims, directing them to their abundant life. Beyond salvation and liberation, he brings tranquility, joy, and gratitude to both sinners and victims as important parts of his atonement. Jesus does these things through the Paraclete. This abundant life consists of *redeemed life* for wrongdoers and *restored life* for victims. The salvation of wrongdoers alone or the liberation of victims alone is unable to bring about abundant life. When these two converge into one, the abundant life will transpire. In Jesus' abundant life, sinners work for the liberation and healing of victims, and victims are involved in the salvation of sinners, thereby enriching each other.

Part 1: Atonement History

1. Irenaeus, *Against Heresies*, vol. 1. Master Christian Library, version 5 (CD-ROM) (Albany, OR: AGES Software, 1997).

2. Ibid.

3. Tertullian, *De fuga in persecutione*, Master Christian Library, 1997.

4. Tertullian, *The Chaplet* or *De corona*, Master Christian Library, 1997.

5. Origen, *Commentaries of Origen: Gospel of John*, book 1, 39, Master Christian Library, 1997.

6. Ibid., book 12, 28.

7. Origen, *Against Celsus*, book 7, 17, Master Christian Library, 1997.

8. Gregory of Nyssa, "The Great Catechism," Master Christian Library, 1997.

9. Augustine, "Sermon," 80, 2, Master Christian Library, 1997.

10. Justin, *The First Apology of Justin*, ch. 63, Master Christian Library, 1997.

11. Justin Martyr, *Dialogue of Justin with Trypho, a Jew*, ch. 100, Master Christian Library, 1997.

12. Irenaeus, *Against Heresies*, book 5, 21, Master Christian Library, 1997.

13. Ibid., book 5, 25.

14. Ibid., book 5, 24.

15. Gustaf Aulén, *Christus Victor: An Historical Study of the Three Main Types of the Idea of Atonement* (London: SPCK, 1953), 20.

16. Ibid., 22.

17. Ibid.

18. Ibid., v.

19. Ibid., 85.

20. Ibid., 135.

21. Ted Peters, *God—the World's Future* (Minneapolis: Fortress Press, 1992), 216.

22. Ibid., 224.

23. Anselm, *Cur Deus Homo,* in *Anselm of Canterbury,* ed. and trans. Jasper Hopkins and Herbert Richardson (Toronto and New York: Edwin Mellen Press, 1974), 102.

24. Ibid.

25. Ibid., 130.

26. Ibid.

27. Ibid., 133.

28. St. Clement, *First Epistle of Clement to the Corinthians,* ch. 7, Master Christian Library, 1997.

29. Peter Abelard, *Peter Abelard's Ethics,* trans. D. E. Luscombe (Oxford: Clarendon Press, 1971), 57.

30. Peter Abelard, *Exposition of the Epistle to the Romans,* excerpted in *A Scholastic Miscellany: Anselm to Ockham,* ed. and trans. Eugene R. Fairweather, Library of Christian Classics (Philadelphia: Westminster Press, 1956), 283.

31. Leif Grane, *Peter Abelard,* trans. Frederick and Christine Crowley (New York: Harcourt, Brace & World, 1970), 101–2.

32. Peter Abelard, *Commentary on the Epistle to the Romans* in *Opera Abelardi,* ed. Cousin (Paris, 1859), 2:207, quoted in A. Victor Murray, *Abelard and St. Bernard: A Study in Twelfth Century "Modernism"* (New York: Manchester University Press, 1967), 130.

33. Ibid., 134.

34. Ibid., 138.

35. Abelard, *Ethics,* 91.

36. J. Denny Weaver, *The Nonviolent Atonement* (Grand Rapids: Wm. B. Eerdmans Publishing Co., 2001), 211.

37. Abelard, *Ethics,* 29.

38. John Calvin, *Institutes of the Christian Religion,* ed. John T. McNeill, trans. Ford Lewis Battles (Philadelphia: Westminster Press, 1960), 2.16.2.

39. Ibid., 2.16.12.

40. Ibid., 2.16.6.

41. Ibid., 2.16.7.

42. Ibid., 2.16.2.

43. Ibid., 2.16.7.

44. Ibid., 2.16.6.

45. Ibid., 2.16.13.

46. Rosemary Radford Ruether, *Women and Redemption: A Theological History* (Minneapolis: Fortress Press, 1998), 279.

47. Rita Nakashima Brock, *Journeys by Heart: A Christology of Erotic Power* (New York: Crossroad, 1988), 56.

48. Delores Williams, *Sisters in the Wilderness: The Challenge of Womanist God-Talk* (Maryknoll, NY: Orbis Books, 1993), 165.

49. Quoted in Leo D. Lefebure, "Beyond Scapegoating: A Conversation with René Girard and Ewert Cousins," *Christian Century* 11 (April 8, 1998): 374.

50. Ibid., 376.

51. René Girard, *I See Satan Fall Like Lightning*, trans. James Williams (Maryknoll, NY: Orbis Books, 2001), 138.

52. Ibid.

53. Ibid., 142.

54. Ibid., 189.

55. Ibid., 151.

56. Ibid., 164.

57. Leo D. Lefebure, "Victims, Violence and the Sacred: Thought of René Girard," *Christian Century* 36 (December 11, 1996): 1229.

58. James Cone, *God of the Oppressed,* rev. ed. (Maryknoll, NY: Orbis Books, 1997), 230–31.

59. Weaver, *Nonviolent Atonement*, 7.

60. Ibid., 8.

61. Ibid., 211.

62. Ibid.

63. J. Denny Weaver, "Christian Faith as Embodied Nonviolence," paper presented at Historic Peace Church Conference, Bienenberg, Switzerland (June 2001), http://www.ajgoddard.net/Ethics_Bibliography/Writers/W/J__Denny_Weaver/j__denny_weaver.html.

64. Karen Baker-Fletcher and Garth Kasimu Baker-Fletcher, *My Sister, My Brother: Womanist and XODUS God-Talk* (Maryknoll, NY: Orbis Books, 1997), 2–3.

65. Weaver, *Nonviolent Atonement*, 20.

66. Weaver, "Christian Faith as Embodied Nonviolence."

67. See Walter Wink, *Naming the Powers: The Language of Power in the New Testament* (Philadelphia: Fortress Press, 1984).

68. Weaver, *Nonviolent Atonement*, 215.

69. Ibid., 75.

70. Ibid., 76.

71. Ibid., 214.

72. Ibid., 220.

73. Paul Tillich, *Dynamics of Faith* (New York: Harper & Row, 1957), 42.

74. Cf. J. E. Cirlot, *A Dictionary of Symbols,* trans. Jack Sage (London: Routledge & Kegan Paul, 1962), 3–11.

75. Tillich, *Dynamics of Faith*, 41.

76. Ibid., 42.

77. Ibid., 42–43.

Part 2: The Triune Atonement

1. Girard has dealt with some issues of the liberation of the oppressed in his book *I See Satan Fall Like Lightning*; however, he needs to connect this insight with his last scapegoat theory. Denny Weaver deals with the issue of victims more than others.

2. I am indebted to my colleague Larry Welborn for this idea.

3. To learn more about *han,* see Andrew Sung Park, *The Wounded Heart of God: The Asian Concept of Han and the Christian Doctrine of Sin* (Nashville: Abingdon Press, 1993).

4. The first two verses are my translations. The third verse is San Kim's translation, quoted in *Suffering and Hope: An Anthology of Asian Writings*, prepared by Ron O'Grady and Lee Soo Jin (Singapore: Christian Conference of Asia, 1978), 35.

5. Ibid., 35, cited by C. S. Song, *Theology from the Womb of Asia* (Maryknoll, NY: Orbis Books, 1986), 97.

6. Song, *Theology from the Womb of Asia,* 98.

7. Although tragedies and natural catastrophes can create *han*, we will limit ourselves to *han* caused by human actions.

8. On this topic, Sharon Thornton is helpful. See her *Broken yet Beloved: A Pastoral Theology of the Cross* (St. Louis: Chalice Press, 2002), 128. Thornton talks about solidarity as "promising, vulnerability, memory, and vision."

9. John Dominic Crossan, *Jesus: A Revolutionary Biography* (San Francisco: HarperSanFrancisco, 1994), 25.

10. John Meier, *A Marginal Jew: Rethinking the Historical Jesus*, vol. 1 (New York: Doubleday, 1991), 6–9, cited in John Dominic Crossan, *The Birth of Christianity* (San Francisco: HarperSanFrancisco, 1998), 350.

11. Cf. Rachel Naomi Remen, *Kitchen Table Wisdom: Stories That Heal* (New York: Riverhead Trade, 1997).

12. Luise Schottroff, "Give to Caesar What Belongs to Caesar and to God What Belongs to God," in *The Love of Enemy and Nonretaliation in the New Testament*, ed. Willard M. Swartley (Louisville, KY: Westminster/ John Knox Press, 1992), 232.

13. Ulrich Luz, *Matthew 1–7* (Minneapolis: Fortress Press, 1989), 325.

14. Jerome H. Neyrey, *Honor and Shame in the Gospel of Matthew* (Louisville, KY: Westminster John Knox Press, 1998), 205.

15. *M. Baba Qamma* 8.6, cited in David Daube, "The Old Testament in the New: A Jewish Perspective," in *Appeasement or Resistance and Other Essays on New Testament Judaism* (Berkeley: University of California Press, 1987), 21. A zuz was an ancient Hebrew silver coin.

16. Walter Wink, *Engaging the Powers: Discernment and Resistance in a World of Domination* (Minneapolis: Fortress Press, 1992), 176.

17. Luise Schottroff, "Non-Violence and the Love of One's Enemies," in *Essays on the Love Commandment*, ed. Luise Schottroff et al., trans. Reginald and Ilse Fuller (Philadelphia: Fortress Press, 1978), 26.

18. Wink, *Engaging the Powers*, 179.

19. Ibid., 182.

20. Ibid.

21. Ibid., 186–89.

22. Ibid., 189.

23. Richard A. Horsley, "Response to Walter Wink," in Swartley, ed., *Love of Enemy and Nonretaliation in the New Testament*, 126–32.

24. Richard A. Horsley, "Ethics and Exegesis," in Swartley, ed., *Love of Enemy and Nonretaliation in the New Testament*, 86–87.

25. Ibid., 130.

26. Walter Wink, "Counterresponse to Richard Horsley," in Swartley, ed., *Love of Enemy and Nonretaliation in the New Testament*, 133–36.

27. Barclay said, "But there were times when a pair of doves would cost as much as 75p inside the Temple and considerably less than 5p outside." William Barclay, *The Gospel of Luke* (Philadelphia: Westminster Press, 1975), 242.

28. John Dominic Crossan, *Who Killed Jesus?* (San Francisco: HarperSanFrancisco, 1995), 64–65.

29. John W. Betlyon, "Coinage," *Anchor Bible Dictionary,* Logos Library System, 1998.

30. According to William Barclay, one *maah* is equivalent to one penny.

31. Barclay, *Gospel of Luke*, 241.

32. BBC, "Who Killed Jesus?" http://www.bbc.co.uk/religion/religions/christianity/history/whokilledjesus_1.shtml.

33. Crossan, *Who Killed Jesus?* 63.

34. William Barclay, *The Gospel of John*, vol. 1 (Philadelphia: Westminster Press, 1975), 113–14.

35. At Passover in 4 BCE after the death of Herod the Great, his son Archelaus massacred three thousand Jews. The following was the occasion. When Jews protested against, grieved over, and made a public clamor for avenging Herod the Great's execution of some teacher, interpreters, and doctors of the law after Herod's death, Archelaus sent in a tribune in command of a cohort with orders to restrain the ringleaders of the sedition and to prevent the spreading of the clamor to the whole crowd. At seeing the troops, the crowd became angry and threw stones at them and killed most of the cohort. Archelaus sent out his entire army to the temple and slew about three thousand of the crowd that were busy with their sacrifices. Crossan, *Who Killed Jesus?* 54–55; Josephus, *The Jewish War* (Grand Rapids: Zondervan, 1982), 2:2–3.

36. Josephus, *Jewish War*, 1:648–55, 6:300–309.

37. Barclay, *Gospel of Luke*, 186.

38. See Andrew Sung Park, *From Hurt to Healing: A Theology of the Wounded*, 133–34.

39. Raymond Brown, *The Gospel according to John* (XIII–XXI), Anchor Bible (Garden City, NY: Doubleday, 1970), 1139.

40. Ibid., 644.

41. Ibid.

42. E. W. Watson, "Introduction," in *The Nicene and Post-Nicene Fathers*, 2nd series, vol. 9, Master Christian Library, version 5 (CD-ROM) (Albany, OR: AGES Software, 1997).

43. St. Hilary of Poitiers, *De Trinitate*, in *The Nicene and Post-Nicene Fathers*, 2nd series, vol. 9, book 8, Master Christian Library, 1997.

44. Subordinationism means that Jesus subordinates to God. Tertullian said, "Clearly, when anything proceeds from a personal subject, and so belongs to him, since it comes from him, it may possibly be such in quality exactly as the personal subject himself is from whom it proceeds, and to whom it belongs." Tertullian, "Against Praxeas," in *The Ante-Nicene Fathers*, vol. 3, ch. 26, Master Christian Library, 1997.

45. Ibid.

46. Ibid., ch. 25.

47. John Ashton, "Paraclete," *Anchor Bible Dictionary* (CD-ROM) (Oak Harbor, WA: Logos Library System, 1998). *Paraclete* is a masculine noun in Greek.

48. Brown, *Gospel according to John (XIII–XXI)*, 1142–43; and Raymond Brown, *The Community of the Beloved Disciple* (New York: Paulist Press, 1979), 139.

49. J. N. Sanders and B. A. Mastin, *A Commentary on the Gospel according to St. John* (Peabody, MA: Hendrickson, 1968), 326.

50. Brown, *Gospel according to John (XIII–XXI)*, 1136.

51. Ibid.

52. Cf. ibid., 1136–37.

53. Ibid., 1137.

54. Rudolf Bultmann, *The Gospel of John: A Commentary*, trans. G. R. Beasley-Murray (Oxford: Basil Blackwell, 1971), 561.

55. Arthur Kleinman, *Patients and Healers in the Context of Culture: An Exploration of the Borderland between Anthropology, Medicine, and Psychiatry*, Comparative Studies of Health Systems and Medical Care (Berkeley: University of California Press, 1980), 72, quoted in Crossan, *Jesus*, 81.

56. Bernhard Anderson, *Understanding the Old Testament* (Upper Saddle River, NJ: Prentice Hall, 1998), 183–84, 359.

57. Ecclesiastes also rejects the retribution theology.

58. George Johnston, *The Spirit-Paraclete in the Gospel of John* (Cambridge: Cambridge University Press, 1970), 50.

59. For Bultmann, sin in this text is unbelief facing the Revealer. See *Gospel of John*, 562.

60. Walter Rauschenbusch, *A Theology for the Social Gospel* (Nashville: Abingdon Press, 1945), 110.

61. Joachim Jeremias, *Jerusalem in the Time of Jesus* (Philadelphia: Fortress Press, 1969), 303f., cited in Byung-mu Ahn, "Jesus and the Minjung," in *Minjung Theology: People as the Subjects of History*, ed. Commission on Theological Concerns of the Christian Conference of Asia (Maryknoll, NY: Orbis Books, 1981), 143.

62. Joachim Jeremias, *New Testament Theology* (New York: Charles Scribner's Sons, 1971), 112.

63. The publicans were particularly despised. They were *toll* collectors (*mōkᵉsā*), different from *tax* collectors (*gabbāyā*). While tax collectors as state officials took in the direct taxes, the toll collectors were subtenants of the rich toll farmers, who had to extract the agreed amount plus their additional profit. They often capitalized on public ignorance

of the scale of tolls to bring money into their pockets during the tax season (Luke 3:12–13). The civil rights of the publicans were denied, and they were deprived of their rights to be witnesses. Joachim Jeremias, *New Testament Theology,* 109–10.

64. Jeremias, *Jerusalem in the Time of Jesus,* 304–6; Byung-mu Ahn, "Jesus and the Minjung," 144.

65. Ahn, "Jesus and the Minjung," 144.

66. Jeremias, *New Testament Theology,* 112.

67. Byung-mu Ahn, "Jesus and the Minjung," 150.

68. Jeremias, *New Testament Theology,* 113.

69. Andrew Sung Park and Susan Nelson, eds., *The Other Side of Sin* (New York: SUNY Press, 2000).

70. Nicholas Wolterstorff, "The Contours of Justice: An Ancient Call for Shalom," in *God and the Victim,* ed. Lisa Lampman (Grand Rapids: Wm. B. Eerdmans Publishing Co., 1999), 123.

71. Ibid., 124.

72. The KJV New Testament Greek Lexicon, "Basileia," http://bible .crosswalk.com/Lexicons/Greek/grk.cgi?number=932&version=kjv.

73. Johnston, *Spirit-Paraclete in the Gospel of John,* 85–86.

74. Bultmann, *Gospel of John,* 565.

75. Paul Tillich, *Systematic Theology,* 3 vols. (Chicago: University of Chicago Press, 1951–1963), 1:283.

76. In the Roman Catholic Church, reconciliation or penance is one of the seven sacraments. The sacrament of penance involves four parts: contrition, confession, absolution, and satisfaction.

77. The Roman Catholic Church furthermore distinguishes perfect contrition from imperfect contrition. The latter, also called attrition, arises out of the fear of punishment and hell. The Roman Catholic position is correct on the idea of contrition that should come out of loving God, rather than fearing hell. The love of God moves us from ourselves to God. It is the change of the heart, not merely change of the mind, denoting the move from us to God. True repentance leads us to love God and thus love others.

78. A. Boyd Luter, "Repentance in the New Testament," *Anchor Bible Dictionary* (CD-ROM) (Oak Harbor, WA: Logos Library System, 1998).

79. James Strong, "ἐπιστρέοω," *The Strongest Strong's Exhaustive Concordance of the Bible* (Grand Rapids: Zondervan, 2001), 1499.

80. Walter Brueggemann, "The Shrill Voices of the Wounded Party," in *The Other Side of Sin: Woundedness from the Perspective of the*

Sinned-Against, ed. Andrew Sung Park and Susan L. Nelson (New York: SUNY Press, 2000), 25–44.

81. God graciously forgave the Ninevites and Israelites at their repentance without punishing them.

82. Jack R. Lundbom, "New Covenant," *Anchor Bible Dictionary,* Logos Library System, 1998.

83. C. M. Tuckett, "Atonement in the New Testament," *Anchor Bible Dictionary,* Logos Library System, 1998.

84. For Jews, salvation is given to them by being descendents of Abraham. The observance of the laws is not the same as being saved, but is a privilege from God to be enjoyed. In the case of Zacchaeus, he became the child of Abraham again through repentance.

85. Allen Reed Millet, *Their War for Korea: American, Asian, and European Combatants and Civilians* (Washington, DC: Brassey's, 2002), 11–13; and In-Yong Lee, "Jesus Math (Matthew 18:21–31)," *Christian Century,* September 6, 2005, 18.

86. Tillich, *Systematic Theology,* 2:165–66.

87. G. W. H. Lampe, "The New Testament Doctrine of *Ktisis,*" *Scottish Journal of Theology* 17 (December 1964): 449.

88. Ibid., 452.

89. H. Paul Santmire, *The Travail of Nature: The Ambiguous Ecological Promise of Christian Theology* (Minneapolis: Fortress Press, 1987). The Priestly writing is the Priestly document, abbreviated as P, which is one of four sources of the Pentateuch, according to the Documentary Hypothesis.

90. Walter Brueggemann, *The Land: Place as Gift, Promise, and Challenge in Biblical Faith* (Philadelphia: Fortress Press, 1977), 3.

91. Claus Westermann, *Blessing: In the Bible and the Life of the Church,* trans. Keith Crim (Philadelphia: Fortress Press, 1978), 4.

92. Santmire, *Travail of Nature,* 191–92.

93. Ibid., 196.

94. Santmire, *Travail of Nature,* 197. "Bless the LORD, O my soul. . . . You are clothed with honor and majesty, wrapped in light as with a garment. You stretch out the heavens like a tent. . . . You cause the grass to grow for the cattle, and plants for people to use, to bring forth food from the earth, and wine to gladden the human heart, oil to make the face shine, and bread to strengthen the human heart" (Ps. 104:1–2, 14–15).

95. H. Paul Santmire, *Nature Reborn: The Ecological and Cosmic Promise of Christian Theology* (Minneapolis: Fortress Press, 2000), 37.

96. Gerhard von Rad, *Genesis,* trans. John H. Marks (Philadelphia: Westminster Press, 1972), cited in Santmire, *Nature Reborn,* 36.

97. Santmire, *Travail of Nature,* 199.

98. Ibid.

99. Edward Schillebeeckx, *Jesus: An Experiment in Christology,* trans. Hubert Hoskins (New York: Crossroads, 1981), cited in Santmire, *Travail of Nature,* 200.

100. William Manson, "Eschatology," *Scottish Journal of Theology Occasional Papers* 2 (1970): 8, 11, 15, cited in Santmire, *Travail of Nature,* 201.

101. Santmire, *Travail of Nature,* 200–218.

102. Ibid., 216–17.

103. Ibid., 217.

104. Ibid.

105. Ibid., 218.

106. John B. Cobb Jr. and David J. Lull, *Romans* (St. Louis: Chalice Press, 2003), 122.

107. Ibid., 123.

108. Lester R. Brown and Sandra Postel, "Thresholds of Change," in *State of the World 1987,* ed. Lester R. Brown (New York: W. W. Norton, 1987), 14.

109. Tim Appenzeller, "The Case of Missing Carbon," *National Geographic,* February 2004, http://magma.nationalgeographic.com/ngm/0402/feature5/index.html.

110. Juliet Eilperin, "World's Power Plant Emissions Detailed: U.S. Appears to Be Worst Carbon Dioxide Polluter, but China Is Catching Up Fast," *Washington Post,* November 15, 2007, A16.

111. Worldwatch Institute, "Climate Change Impacts Rise," *Vital Signs,* July 7, 2006, http://www.worldwatch.org/node/4249.

112. "Global Warming Fast Facts," National Geographic News, June 14, 2007, http://news.nationalgeographic.com/news/2004/12/1206_041206_global_warming.html.

113. *IPCC Fourth Assessment Report,* Topic 1, November 17, 2007, http://www.ipcc.ch/pdf/assessment-report/ar4/syr/ar4_syr_topic1.pdf.

114. Juliet Eilperin, "Antarctic Ice Sheet Is Melting Rapidly: New Study Warns of Rising Sea Levels," *Washington Post,* March 3, 2006, A1.

115. United Nations Development Programme, "Climate Change Will Sabotage Indonesia's Fight against Poverty: UNDP Report Focuses on the Forgotten Story of Climate Change," press release, November

27, 2007, http://www.undp.or.id/press/view.asp?FileID=20071127-2& lang=en.

116. Lori Brown, "State of the World: A Year in Review," in *State of the World 2004,* ed. Linda Starke (New York: W. W. Norton, 2004), xxii.

117. William Grimes, "If Chickens Are So Smart, Why Aren't They Eating Us?" Late Edition, *New York Times,* January 12, 2003.

118. Karen Davis, *Prisoned Chickens, Poisoned Eggs: An Inside Look at the Modern Poultry Industry* (Summertown, TN: Book Publishing Co., 1996), 57, 91–92.

119. Pamela Bowers, "A Diagnostic Dilemma," *Poultry Marketing and Technology,* August-September 1993, 18–19.

120. Lisa Duchene, "Are Pigs Smarter than Dogs?" in *Research Penn State,* June 16, 2008, http://www.rps.psu.edu/probing/pigs.html.

121. Danielle Nierenberg, "Rethinking the Global Meat Industry," in *State of the World 2006* (New York: W. W. Norton, 2006), 29.

122. Bernard E. Rollin and Robert Desch, "Farm Factories," in *Christian Century* 35 (December 19, 2001), 26. Rollin is University Distinguished Professor of Philosophy, Physiology, and Animal Sciences at Colorado State University in Fort Collins.

123. Nierenberg, "Rethinking the Global Meat Industry," 29.

124. Rollin and Desch, "Farm Factories," 26.

125. Nierenberg, "Rethinking the Global Meat Industry," 29.

126. T. G. Nagaraja and M. M. Chengappa, "Liver Abscesses in Feedlot Cattle: A Review," *Journal of Animal Science* 76, no. 1 (1998): 287–98.

127. Rollin and Desch, "Farm Factories," 27.

128. Leo Horrigan, Robert S. Lawrence, and Polly Walker, "How Sustainable Agriculture Can Address the Environmental and Human Health Harms of Industrial Agriculture," *Environmental Health Perspectives* 5 (May 2002): 454.

129. Nierenberg, "Rethinking the Global Meat Industry," 39.

130. 'Scientists: Factory Farming Drop Could End Mad Cow," *CNN,* December 4, 2000, http://archives.cnn.com/2000/HEALTH/ 12/04/health.madcow.reut/index.html.

131. "EU Tackles BSE Crisis," *BBC News,* November 29, 2000, http://news.bbc.co.uk/2/hi/europe/1046184.stm.

132. The passages of Gen. 9:9–13 belong to the Priestly tradition.

133. Santmire, *Nature Reborn,* 44. I changed "the Father" to "God."

134. I changed "the Lord" to "God" and "his" to "your."

Selected Bibliography

Abelard, Peter. *Exposition of the Epistle to the Romans.* Excerpted in *A Scholastic Miscellany: Anselm to Ockham*, edited and translated by Eugene R. Fairweather, Library of Christian Classics. Philadelphia: Westminster Press, 1956.

———. *Peter Abelard's Ethics.* Translated by D. E. Luscombe. Oxford: Clarendon Press, 1971.

Anderson, Bernhard. *Understanding the Old Testament.* Upper Saddle River, NJ: Prentice Hall, 1998.

Anselm of Canterbury. *Cur Deus Homo.* In *Anselm of Canterbury*, edited and translated by Jasper Hopkins and Herbert Richardson. Toronto and New York: Edwin Mellen Press, 1974.

Ashton, John. "Paraclete." *Anchor Bible Dictionary.* CD-ROM. Oak Harbor, WA: Logos Library System, 1998.

Augustine of Hippo. *Our Lord's Sermon on the Mount.* In Master Christian Library. CD-ROM, version 5. Albany, OR: AGES Software, 1997.

Aulén, Gustaf. *Christus Victor: An Historical Study of the Three Main Types of the Idea of Atonement.* London: SPCK, 1953.

Baker-Fletcher, Karen, and Garth Kasimu Baker-Fletcher. *My Sister, My Brother: Womanist and XODUS God-Talk.* Maryknoll, NY: Orbis Books, 1997.

Barclay, William. *The Gospel of Luke.* Philadelphia: Westminster Press, 1975.

Berry, R. J. E., ed. *Environmental Stewardship: Critical Perspective, Past and Present.* London and New York: T. & T. Clark, 2006.

Borg, Marcus, and N. T. Wright. *The Meaning of Jesus: Two Visions.* San Francisco: HarperSanFrancisco, 1999.

Brock, Rita Nakashima. *Journeys by Heart: A Christology of Erotic Power.* New York: Crossroad, 1988.

Brock, Rita Nakashima, and Rebecca Ann Parker. *Proverbs of Ashes.* Boston: Beacon Press, 2001.

Brown, Joanne Carlson, and Carole R. Bohn, ed. *Christianity, Patriarchy, and Abuse: A Feminist Critique.* New York: Pilgrim Press, 1989.

Brown, Joanne Carlson, and Rebecca Parker. "For God So Loved the World?" In *Christianity, Patriarchy, and Abuse: A Feminist Critique*, edited by Joanne Carlson Brown and Carole R. Bohn, 1–30. New York: Pilgrim Press, 1989.

Brown, Lester, ed. *State of the World 1987*. New York: W. W. Norton, 1987.

Brown, Raymond. *The Community of the Beloved Disciple*. New York: Paulist Press, 1979.

———. *The Gospel according to John (XIII–XXI)*. Anchor Bible. Garden City, NY: Doubleday, 1970.

Brueggemann, Walter. *The Land: Place as Gift, Promise, and Challenge in Biblical Faith*. Philadelphia: Fortress Press, 1977.

Bultmann, Rudolf. *The Gospel of John: A Commentary*. Translated by G. R. Beasley-Murray. Oxford: Basil Blackwell, 1971.

Calvin, John. *Institutes of the Christian Religion*. Edited by John T. McNeill. Translated by Ford Lewis Battles. Philadelphia: Westminster Press, 1960.

Chung, Hyun Kyung, *Struggle to Be the Sun Again*. Maryknoll, NY: Orbis Books, 1990.

Cobb, John B., Jr. *Christ in a Pluralistic Age*. Philadelphia: Westminster Press, 1975.

———. *Is It Too Late? A Theology of Ecology*. Denton, TX: Environmental Ethics Books, 1995.

Cobb, John B., Jr., and David J. Lull. *Romans*. St. Louis: Chalice Press, 2003.

Cone, James H. *God of the Oppressed*. Rev. ed. Maryknoll, NY: Orbis Books, 1997.

Crossan, John Dominic. *The Birth of Christianity*. San Francisco: HarperSanFrancisco, 1998.

———. *Jesus: A Revolutionary Biography*. San Francisco: HarperSanFrancisco, 1994.

———. *Who Killed Jesus?* San Francisco: HarperSanFrancisco, 1995.

Daube, David. *Appeasement or Resistance and Other Essays on New Testament Judaism*. Berkeley: University of California Press, 1987.

Davis, Karen. *Prisoned Chickens, Poisoned Eggs: An Inside Look at the Modern Poultry Industry*. Summertown, TN: Book Publishing Co., 1996.

Douglas, Kelly Brown. *The Black Christ*. Maryknoll, NY: Orbis Books, 1994.

Girard, René. *I See Satan Fall Like Lightning*. Maryknoll, NY: Orbis Books, 2001.

————. *The Scapegoat.* Translated by Yvonne Freccero. Baltimore: Johns Hopkins University Press, 1986.

Grane, Leif. *Peter Abelard.* Translated by Frederick and Christine Crowley. New York: Harcourt, Brace & World, 1970.

Green, Joel B., and Mark D. Baker. *Recovering the Scandal of the Cross.* Downers Grove, IL: InterVarsity Press, 2000.

Gregory of Nyssa. *The Great Catechism.* In Master Christian Library. CD-ROM, version 5. Albany, OR: AGES Software, 1997.

Heim, S. Mark. *Saved from Sacrifice: A Theology of the Cross.* Grand Rapids: Wm. B. Eerdmans Publishing Co., 2001.

Inbody, Tyron L. *The Many Faces of Christology.* Nashville: Abingdon Press, 2002.

IPCC Fourth Assessment Report, Topic 1. November 17, 2007. http://www.ipcc.ch/pdf/assessment-report/ar4/syr/ar4_syr_topic1.pdf.

Irenaeus. *Against Heresies.* In Master Christian Library. CD-ROM, version 5. Albany, OR: AGES Software, 1997.

Jeremias, Joachim. *Jerusalem in the Time of Jesus.* Philadelphia: Fortress Press, 1969.

Josephus. *Jewish War.* Grand Rapids: Zondervan, 1982.

Justin. *Dialogue of Justin with Trypho, a Jew.* Master Christian Library. 1997.

————. *The First Apology of Justin.* In Master Christian Library. CD-ROM, version 5. Albany, OR: AGES Software, 1997.

Keener, Craig S. *Gift Giver: The Holy Spirit for Today.* Grand Rapids: Baker, 2001.

Kleinman, Arthur. *Patients and Healers in the Context of Culture: An Exploration of the Borderland between Anthropology, Medicine, and Psychiatry.* Berkeley: University of California Press, 1980.

Lefebure, Leo D. "Beyond Scapegoating: A Conversation with René Girard and Ewert Cousins." *Christian Century* 11 (April 8, 1998): 372–75.

————. "Victims, Violence, and the Sacred: Thought of René Girard." *Christian Century* 36 (December 11, 1996): 1226–29.

Luter, A. Boyd. "Repentance in the New Testament." *Anchor Bible Dictionary.* CD-ROM. Oak Harbor, WA: Logos Library System, 1998.

Luz, Ulrich. *Matthew 1–7.* Minneapolis: Fortress Press, 1989.

McDaniel, Jay. *With Roots and Wings: Christianity in an Age of Ecology and Dialogue.* Maryknoll, NY: Orbis Books, 1995.

Meier, John. *A Marginal Jew: Rethinking the Historical Jesus.* 3 vols. New York: Doubleday, 1991–1994.

Murray, A. Victor. *Abelard and St. Bernard: A Study in Twelfth Century "Modernism."* New York: Manchester University Press, 1967.

Neyrey, Jerome H. *Honor and Shame in the Gospel of Matthew.* Louisville, KY: Westminster John Knox Press, 1998.

Nierenberg, Danielle. "Rethinking the Global Meat Industry." In *State of the World 2006,* 24–40. New York: W. W. Norton, 2006.

Origen, *Commentaries of Origen.* In Master Christian Library. CD-ROM, version 5. Albany, OR: AGES Software, 1997.

———. *Against Celsus.* In Master Christian Library. CD-ROM, version 5. Albany, OR: AGES Software, 1997.

Park, Andrew Sung. *From Hurt to Healing: A Theology of the Wounded.* Nashville: Abingdon Press, 2004.

———. *The Wounded Heart of God: The Asian Concept of Han and the Christian Doctrine of Sin.* Nashville: Abingdon Press, 1993.

Park, Andrew Sung, and Susan L. Nelson, eds. *The Other Side of Sin.* New York: SUNY Press, 2000.

Peters, Ted. *God—the World's Future.* Minneapolis: Fortress Press, 2000.

Ruether, Rosemary Radford. *Women and Redemption: A Theological History.* Minneapolis: Fortress Press, 1998.

Sanders, J. N., and B. A. Mastin. *A Commentary on the Gospel according to St. John.* Peabody, MA: Hendrickson, 1968.

Santmire, H. Paul. *Nature Reborn: The Ecological and Cosmic Promise of Christian Theology.* Minneapolis: Fortress Press, 2000.

———. *The Travail of Nature: The Ambiguous Ecological Promise of Christian Theology.* Minneapolis: Fortress Press, 1987.

Schott, James. *Domination and the Arts of Resistance: Hidden Transcripts.* New Haven, CT: Yale University Press, 1992.

Schottroff, Luise, R. H. Fuller, C. Burchard, and M. J. Suggs. *Essays on the Love Commandment.* Translated by Reginald and Ilse Fuller. Philadelphia: Fortress Press, 1978.

Starke, Linda, ed. *State of the World 2004.* New York: W. W. Norton, 2004.

St. Clement. *First Epistle of Clement to the Corinthians.* In Master Christian Library. CD-ROM, version 5. Albany, OR: AGES Software, 1997.

Swartley, Willard M., ed. *The Love of Enemy and Nonretaliation in the New Testament.* Louisville, KY: Westminster/John Knox Press, 1992.

Tertullian. *The Chaplet, or De corona.* In Master Christian Library. CD-ROM, version 5. Albany, OR: AGES Software, 1997.

———. *De fuga in persecutione.* In Master Christian Library. CD-ROM, version 5. Albany, OR: AGES Software, 1997.

Thornton, Sharon G. *Broken yet Beloved: A Pastoral Theology of the Cross.* St. Louis: Chalice Press, 2002.

Tillich, Paul. *Dynamics of Faith.* New York: Harper & Row, 1957.

Trelstad, Marit A., ed. *Cross Examinations: Readings on the Meaning of the Cross Today.* Minneapolis: Fortress Press, 2006.

Trocmé, André. *Jesus and the Nonviolent Revolution.* Edited by Charles Moore. Maryknoll, NY: Orbis Books, 2003.

United Nations Development Programme, "Climate Change Will Sabotage Indonesia's Fight against Poverty: UNDP Report Focuses on the Forgotten Story of Climate Change" (press release). November 27, 2007. http://www.undp.or.id/press/view.asp?FileID=20071127–2 &lang=en.

Vickers, Jason E. *Invocation and Assent: The Making and the Remaking of Trinitarian Theology.* Grand Rapids: Wm. B. Eerdmans Publishing Co., 2008.

Weaver, J. Denny. "Christian Faith as Embodied Nonviolence." Paper presented at Historic Peace Church Conference, Bienenberg, Switzerland (June 2001). http://www.ajgoddard.net/Ethics_Bibliography/Writers/W/J__Denny_Weaver/j__denny_weaver.html.

———. *The Nonviolent Atonement.* Grand Rapids: Wm. B. Eerdmans Publishing Co., 2001.

———. "Violence in Christian Theology." In *Teaching Peace: Nonviolence and the Liberal Arts,* edited by J. Denny Weaver and Gerald Biesecker-Mast, 39–52. Lanham, MD: Rowman & Littlefield, 2003.

Westhelle, Vitor. *The Scandalous God: The Use and Abuse of the Cross.* Minneapolis: Fortress Press, 2006.

Williams, Delores. "Black Women's Surrogacy Experience and the Christian Notion of Redemption." In *Cross Examinations: Readings on the Meaning of the Cross Today,* edited by Marit A. Trelstad, 19–32. Minneapolis: Fortress Press, 2006.

———. *Sisters in the Wilderness: The Challenge of Womanist God-Talk.* Maryknoll, NY: Orbis Books, 1993.

Wink, Walter. *Engaging the Powers: Discernment and Resistance in a World of Domination.* Minneapolis: Fortress Press, 1992.

———. *Naming the Powers: The Language of Power in the New Testament.* Philadelphia: Fortress Press, 1984.

Index